Cinderella Man

Written By
MARC CERASINI
Based on the Motion Picture Screenplay By
CLIFF HOLLINGSWORTH and AKIVA GOLDSMAN
Motion Picture Story By
CLIFF HOLLINGSWORTH

Level 4

Retold by Paul Shipton
Series Editors: Andy Hopkins and Jocelyn Potter

Pearson Education Limited

Edinburgh Gate, Harlow,
Essex CM20 2JE, England
and Associated Companies throughout the world.

ISBN 978-1-4058-8208-8

First published 2006
This edition published 2008

1 3 5 7 9 10 8 6 4 2

Text copyright © Pearson Education Ltd 2008

Typeset by Graphicraft Limited, Hong Kong
Set in 11/14pt Bembo
Printed in China
SWTC/01

Produced for the Publishers by
Graphicraft Productions Limited, Dartford, UK

Published by Pearson Education Limited in association with
Penguin Books Ltd, both companies being subsidiaries of Pearson Plc

Acknowledgement

Photograph page: viii © ® Estate of James J. Braddock

For a complete list of the titles available in the Penguin Readers series please write to your local
Pearson Education office or to: Penguin Readers Marketing Department, Pearson Education,
Edinburgh Gate, Harlow, Essex, CM20 2JE

Contents

Introduction

As Jim Braddock stepped out into the bright lights, the crowd became silent. The ring seemed so far away. Between him and it were thousands of people—Jim's people. He knew the looks on their faces—people who saw no chance of a future. Some had spent their last dollar to be here, but tonight they all held their heads high. Their eyes followed him with the wild hope that the story of the Cinderella Man would have a happy ending.

The story of heavyweight boxer James J. Braddock—the "Cinderella Man"—is a true one. It begins in New York City in the late 1920s. The 1920s had seen good times in the United States. The rest of the world watched as taller and taller buildings were built in cities like New York. More and more Americans were buying Henry Ford's cars, and Hollywood was making movies that were seen around the world. In the country's big cities, it was a time of new fashions, new machines, and exciting new music.

President Herbert Hoover thought that the good times would never end, but he was wrong. The country was producing more than it needed, and many historians believe that this was the cause of the problem. There were still many poor people in the United States—almost half the population—and these people couldn't afford to buy new things. At the same time, the country's rich people couldn't continue to buy things they already owned. The end came suddenly, in October 1929, when the whole system crashed. The economy failed, banks closed, families around the country lost their money, and millions of people lost their jobs and their homes. In 1932, the country voted for a popular new president, Franklin Delano Roosevelt, who worked hard to solve the country's problems. There were no quick answers, though—in

1933, there were 15 million people without jobs in the country, one in every four working people—and the 1930s continued to be hard for many Americans.

The true story of Jim Braddock was similar to the story of many Americans. He made a lot of money in the 1920s as a successful boxer, and he and his family had everything they wanted. But for Braddock, too, the good times couldn't last. He lost all of his money in 1929, and he experienced bad luck in his professional life when he began to lose fights. Like many Americans, Braddock had to take any work he could find. He had to fight just to put food on the table for his family. Most people believed that his life as a professional heavyweight boxer had ended. The story of his second chance is one of the sport's greatest stories.

It was a story that the writer and boxing supporter Cliff Hollingsworth knew well. Thinking that it would make a great movie, he spoke to Jim Braddock's sons in 1994. They told him that their father had been a national hero, but that now most people hadn't heard of him. Hollingsworth wanted to change that situation so "this forgotten hero will be remembered once again."

Actor Russell Crowe became interested in making a movie of Braddock's story. Crowe, who was born in New Zealand and grew up in Australia, told how Braddock did everything possible to support his family. "I just wanted people to hear this true American story," said the actor.

Filmmaker Ron Howard learned more about the possible movie when he made A *Beautiful Mind* with Russell Crowe. Howard already knew about Braddock—when he was little, his father had told him about the fighter.

It was clear to the filmmakers that Braddock's wife and family were the most important things in his world, so they knew that the character of Jim's wife, Mae, was very important to the movie. Actress Renée Zellweger was interested in playing Mae because

Mae was a strong woman at a time when many women had no voice at all. "She's never afraid to tell Jim what's in her heart, even when it's not what he wants to hear," said Zellweger.

Before the movie could be made, Russell Crowe had a lot of work to do. After his last movie, the actor weighed 103 kilograms. Jim Braddock fought at 81 kilograms and he was taller than Crowe, so the actor had to lose weight. He did this by methods from Braddock's days—swimming, running, riding a bicycle, and climbing.

He also had to study boxing, working long hours at the punching bag and in the ring. He was helped by the most famous trainer in boxing's history, Angelo Dundee, who has worked with Sugar Ray Leonard, Mike Tyson, and the greatest champion of them all, Muhammad Ali. The trainer helped Crowe to box, and to box just like Jim Braddock. Dundee spoke of the actor's speed and skill in the ring. "Best of all, he has learned to think like a fighter," said the famous trainer.

Crowe was also not afraid of pain. He was knocked down several times and suffered loose and broken teeth; one week before filming began, his shoulder was badly hurt. When the movie was made, some of Braddock's opponents were played by real boxers, who had to learn to throw punches that didn't hurt so much. They didn't always remember! In one scene, boxer Mark Simmons hit Crowe so hard that actor Paul Giamatti, playing Braddock's manager, heard the boxing glove hit Crowe's head. Giamatti's look of shock in the film wasn't acting! "I don't know how he continued with the fight," said Giamatti.

In the end, *Cinderella Man* is not just a story about boxing. It is the story of a family who stayed together in hard times—the story of a man who fought for what he loved and believed in.

James J. Braddock

Chapter 1   A Lucky Man

Madison Square Garden, New York, November 30, 1928

There were nineteen thousand boxing supporters around the center ring in Madison Square Garden, and most were waiting for just one thing—for one fighter to murder another. Tonight they were waiting for Gerald "Tuffy" Griffiths, the "Terror from out West," to destroy New Jersey's Jim Braddock.

At the sound of the bell, Braddock stood under the hot lights and watched Griffiths rush out into the ring. Tuffy Griffiths had come to New York after winning fifty fights. He had won his last fight with a knockout in the first round. Everybody knew that he would do the same to Braddock—everybody except Braddock and his manager, Joe Gould. Gould believed in Braddock.

A sudden jab from Braddock knocked Griffiths back. The fighters started moving around the ring, throwing and blocking punches. Griffiths threw the same punches that had easily beaten his other opponents, but Braddock stayed on his feet. Blood and sweat poured into his eyes.

None of the reporters around the ring expected the New Jersey boxer to reach the end of the second round. But by round two, Braddock had timed his opponent's rushes. Within one minute, he hit Griffiths with his big punch—his right cross—and Tuffy went down. The crowd stood, shouting. But the referee had only counted to three before Griffiths was back on his feet and the fight continued.

Time stretched for Braddock now, and his opponent's slightest move seemed enormous. Braddock paid no attention to the screams of the crowd, to the pain he felt. This was his chance to finish Griffiths. He threw his big right punch again, and again Tuffy was on the floor.

"One . . . two . . . three . . . four . . ." the referee counted.

For a second time, Griffiths got to his feet. But Braddock was ready, stepping in close and throwing punch after punch. Then his right hand flew forward and found Griffiths' chin for the last time. The big fighter hit the floor again. He tried to stand, but his legs were like rubber. No more punches hit him, but he went down—and stayed down.

"And from the great state of New Jersey, by a knockout, tonight's light heavyweight winner . . . Jim Braddock!"

The crowd was back on its feet. The local boy had won! Braddock had been born in Hell's Kitchen, a poor neighborhood of New York just a stone's throw from Madison Square Garden. Braddock punched the air in celebration. He looked at the crowd, at the men in their suits and ties and the women with their fashionable haircuts and expensive clothes. It was Friday night, the world seemed to be having a party, and Jim Braddock's win was one more reason to celebrate!

Griffiths was Braddock's eighteenth knockout since his first professional fight in 1926. His twenty-seventh win. The fight organizers had had big plans for Griffiths. After this surprise win, maybe Braddock would have his chance to fight for the title of heavyweight champion. That was every boxer's dream.

Inside the ring, Joe Gould rushed out of the corner and jumped onto his boxer's back. Both men looked at the crowd and listened to its shouts. Jim smiled. He was *a winner . . .*

♦

The tall boxer and his manager stepped out through the side entrance into a crowd of about a hundred well-dressed supporters.

"Just sign your name for a few of them," said Joe. "Leave them wanting more."

"Do you want to sign my name for me, too?" Jim asked his manager with a smile.

People crowded around Jim. He liked them; he liked the fact that they loved him.

"You win some, you lose some, Johnston," said Joe.

Jim looked up. His manager was talking to a big man who had come out of the same side entrance. Jimmy Johnston organized the fights at Madison Square Garden. No boxer fought there without his permission. Johnston and men like him ruled the world of boxing. Tonight Johnston had wanted Griffiths to win the fight. Braddock was supposed to be an easy win for Griffiths.

Jim touched his manager's arm. "Leave it," he said.

But Joe continued talking. "Maybe you support the wrong guys? Griffiths was heavier than my boy, and what happened? Jab, cross . . ."

"Actually, it was jab, jab, cross," said Jim. He didn't like to see Joe arguing with a man as powerful as Johnston. But the little manager had always supported Jim, and the fighter couldn't let his manager stand alone now.

"Jab, jab, cross!" repeated Joe. "And then your boy's out! So maybe no one's a *loser*? Right, Johnston?"

Loser. Jim hated that word. Some people had said that his early opponents were no good. Easy fights. Losers. So what did that make Jim? But after tonight . . . after Griffiths . . . what could they say now?

Joe Gould and Jimmy Johnston stared hard at each other. Just like inside the boxing ring, time seemed to stretch. And then Johnston turned and walked to his waiting car.

Jim shook his head. His little manager had no control over his mouth. "I'll get us a taxi," he said.

But Joe pointed to a big, shiny new car across the street. "You have to show you're doing well," he said. The manager organized his life by this belief—expensive clothes, the best restaurants, and now this car. A uniformed driver opened the back door, and the two men got in.

Through the car's windows, New York seemed alive. The city's bright lights shone and people laughed and talked as they went to shows and clubs. It was an exciting time to live in the city. Tall buildings were going up everywhere, and everybody seemed to be getting rich. Jim Braddock and Joe Gould wanted a piece of that success, too. They had even started their own taxi company.

"Let's go to a club," said Joe. "You should be seen in the right places . . ."

But Jim just said, "Home, Joe."

With a shake of his head, Joe told the driver, and the car turned toward New Jersey. This had been Jim's home since soon after his birth. His parents had moved from Ireland to New York, looking for a better life. Later, for the same reason, they had moved their family across the Hudson River to New Jersey.

Here Jim had grown up a typical American boy. By the time he stopped going to school, his older brother had started to box. One day he and Jim began to argue, and soon they were fighting. Although his brother was bigger and had much more experience, Jim didn't do badly. That's when he realized—maybe he could be a winner in the boxing ring.

Not long after this, he had first met Joe Gould in a local gym. Joe needed someone to train with one of his boxers, and he offered five dollars to the tall teenager. Jim had gone into the ring and given Gould's boxer a lesson. The manager had stayed with Jim since then, through one hundred amateur fights, and then through all his professional fights.

Now the car turned onto Jim's tree-lined street in a nice, quiet neighborhood of Newark, New Jersey's biggest city. Joe pulled some cash out of his pocket and began to count out Jim's share of the prize money.

"Do you want to come in?" asked Jim as the car stopped outside his house. "The kids would love to see you."

Joe paused. "Are you still married to the same girl?"

"I was this morning," answered Jim.

"I'll come in another time," said Joe. "And tell her I didn't charge you for the towels."

As Jim climbed out, he forced himself not to laugh. Joe Gould was afraid of nothing in the world of boxing, but he turned and ran from Jim's wife, Mae, with her hard questions about the prize money and Jim's share of it.

The front door of the house was open now, and there, in the golden light of the hall, was Mae. Her pale face was serious as she waited. From the first time he had met her, Jim had loved her. He moved toward her now, telling himself he was a lucky man to have a wife like Mae.

◆

When Mae Braddock saw her husband, the dark cloud of worry disappeared. She could breathe again. Feel again.

Fight night was always like this for Mae. In the afternoon, Jimmy kissed her goodbye. Then she just watched the clock and hoped that he was safe. The long hours full of fear only ended when Jim came home.

She knew that men died in the ring. Not often, but it happened. And if they didn't die, they were hurt, badly. Mae didn't understand the sport. To her it was a world of pain and danger. But she loved her husband, and so she tried to support him.

Mae Theresa Fox had grown up near the Braddock family in New Jersey. She had always liked big Jim Braddock, and he loved Mae from the time he first met her. But Jim was shy, and it took him a long time to ask Mae to marry him. He said that he wanted to wait until he had enough money to buy a nice home. When he had $30,000 from his prize money—a small fortune—he finally asked. As he waited nervously for her answer, Mae noticed the sweat on Jim's face. She couldn't stop herself from laughing. The money didn't matter to her—of course she would marry him!

Now Mae looked at her husband. She knew that Griffiths had been expected to win tonight's fight. Her eyes asked the question, and Jim's answer was a slow shake of the head. Mae looked away. She hated to see Jimmy in pain—that's why she never went to the fights—and she hated to see him like this. But then she looked up and saw Jimmy smile. He had won!

"I could kill you," said Mae, kissing her husband.

Jim's two sons ran into the hall. They jumped around their father's legs, shouting with excitement.

"Daddy, did you win?" cried four-year-old Jay.

Howard, who was only three, was just happy that Daddy was home. Jim picked the boys up and kissed them. *My little men*, he thought. His eyes met Mae's. *My little family*.

Jim told them all about the fight, acting it out punch by punch. It wasn't easy for Mae to put the boys to bed after that. When she had checked their sleeping baby girl, Rosy, she sat down to eat dinner with Jimmy.

"So did Griffiths have a big punch?" she asked.

"You could come and watch me fight," suggested Jim.

But Mae looked away. "You get punched, and it feels like *I'm* getting punched. But I'm not as strong as you . . ." She forced herself to smile. "And who wants newspaper stories about me running out from a fight again?"

Jim remembered when this had happened. His opponent had knocked him down that day, and Mae had seen it. Jim still remembered the look of fear on her face. It didn't seem to matter that Jim had won the fight in the end. After that, Mae bravely continued coming to watch Jim box. He didn't know how painful it was for her until a few fights later. Jim was having a bad night and he took a lot of punishment. Not able to watch anymore, Mae had run off before the final bell. A reporter saw her go, and the story was in the newspapers. Mae never went to a fight again.

Now she looked at her husband. "Were there any girls waiting outside after the fight?"

"Maybe," said Jim with a smile.

Mae moved around the table. She spoke in a different voice now, pretending to be one of the women. "Oh, Mr. Braddock," she said. "You're so strong. Your hands are so big."

Mae moved in close, and she wasn't joking now when she said, "I am so proud of you, Jimmy."

That night, as he got ready for bed, Jim stood in the bedroom of his beautiful home. He looked at their wedding picture. Then he took off the gold cross from around his neck and kissed it, looking at his own face in the mirror. It was the face of a lucky man. A lucky man and a winner.

Chapter 2   Hard Times

Newark, New Jersey, September 25, 1933

Jim Braddock looked through the drawers below the same mirror that had shown him the face of a lucky man. Dressing was quick these days: he just put on what Mae had washed or fixed the night before. He didn't have to kiss his gold cross for luck. He had sold it years ago. Everyone's luck had gone now—even Jim Braddock's.

Something moved outside the window, probably a rat. This was just a part of life when you lived in a single room in a dirty, crowded apartment building. Behind Jim, his three hungry children shared a bed in the cold family bedroom. Mae had hung a blanket across the room to turn one room into two.

He looked again at his and Mae's wedding picture. In the last few years they had lost their house and most of their furniture, but they would always have this. In the picture, Mae looked beautiful; Jim stood next to her, wearing a suit he didn't own now. The couple in the photo smiled, not knowing the hard future that was ahead. But Jim liked to look at the picture every day. It reminded him of the good things in his life.

He stepped into the kitchen, where Mae was cooking breakfast. She looked different now—thinner, with dark circles under her eyes. But to Jim she was still beautiful.

"I can't find my socks," he said.

"Jim!" whispered Mae, but it was too late.

"Mom, I want to eat, too," said little Rosy, pushing through the blanket. Mae began to cut another thin piece of meat.

"Sorry," said Jim.

Rosy couldn't remember living in a big house, surrounded by nice things, with new clothes and plenty of food. The girl climbed onto her father, and Jim held her close to him. He hated seeing his children grow up like this; it was harder than any fight.

"We got a final bill," said Mae, "for the gas and electricity."

Jim's shoulders fell. He took down a jar from the shelf, where they kept their money for a "rainy day." He shook it and listened to the few coins in the jar.

"It's clearly been raining more than I thought recently," he said.

Mae picked up three dishes and put a thin piece of hot meat on each one. Jim began to cut up his daughter's food.

"I'm fighting Abe Feldman tonight," he told his wife. He didn't tell her that Feldman had lost only one fight in nineteen. Instead, he told her what he would earn—fifty dollars, more than he could earn in one whole week on the docks.

Mae couldn't hide the old fear in her eyes. Since hard times had hit their family—and the whole country—she had started to hate the ring, with its punishments and its empty promises.

"Mommy, I want some more," said Rosy.

Jim looked at Mae and Rosy with their empty plates. "Mae, I had a dream last night," he said, standing from the table. "I dreamed that I was having dinner at an expensive hotel, and I had a big, thick steak." He put on his old coat. "I had so much food,

I'm just not hungry now." He spoke more quietly to his daughter. "Can you help me? Mommy cooked this, and I don't want to hurt her feelings."

Rosy wasn't sure whether to believe him, but Jim moved the meat from his plate to hers. With wide eyes, the child immediately began to eat.

"Jimmy—" Mae began, but he silenced her with a kiss.

You can't work on an empty stomach, her eyes said to him.

Jim's answer was simple. "You're my girls."

When Jim stepped outside, he remembered that things weren't so bad for him and his family. Times were even harder for many other people. He walked past old, broken cars next to trash can fires. Those useless cars were homes now, homes to people with no jobs and no hopes.

This part of Newark was very different from Jim's old leafy neighborhood. Most of the dirty brown and gray buildings around here had broken windows and paint coming off. Most of the stores were closed, and garbage cans lay empty in the street. People threw nothing away these days.

Ten thousand factories in the New York area had been closed down. Everywhere Jim looked, he saw people without jobs. Businessmen, teachers, office workers, lawyers, bankers . . . all were looking for work. There were men in four-year-old suits, happy to clean a yard for a dollar. Others stood in line at employment offices from morning until night.

Disaster had struck on October 29, 1929. Some people called it Black Tuesday, others the Crash. It was the end of America's good times in the 1920s. The economy failed, and suddenly millions of people were out of work. At first, Jim thought that the problem wouldn't last long. But then his bank closed and his taxi company went out of business. By 1932, the Braddocks had lost every cent of Jim's boxing money.

New York wasn't a city of bright lights and happy party-goers now. The city was filled with a gray crowd of people without hope. They stood in endless lines for soup or bread; they froze on street corners; they looked for work and found none. Hungry, empty, hopeless people.

Jim's only hope had been boxing. The prize money was less, but boxing was still popular, cheap entertainment. But, after the crash, Jim's success as a boxer had ended. In 1930, '31, '32—and now 1933—he lost more fights than he won. It was harder and harder for Gould to get him good fights.

Jim had to look for other work. With so many factories closed, he tried Newark's busy docks. Early every morning, he joined the crowd looking for work there. In the dark and the cold, they waited by the locked gate of a high fence.

At last, the foreman pulled open the gate. He looked at the tired, hungry faces of the men there. This man had the power of life or death; he could change the luck of every man here.

"I need nine men," he said.

Men began pushing forward—*Me! Pick me!*—as the foreman counted out workers. "One, two, three . . ." Jim pushed forward, too, but then: ". . . nine."

Jim closed his eyes. After all of that waiting, it had ended in less than thirty seconds. He hadn't been picked.

"I've been here since four o'clock," said a man's voice.

The man had stepped forward to complain. Jim had spoken to him once. His name was Ben and, like Jim, he had a wife and three kids to support.

The foreman began to turn away, but suddenly Ben was holding a gun and pointing it at the foreman's heart. His hand shook and his eyes were wild. "I was here first."

The foreman lifted his eyes from the gun to Ben's face. "My mistake," he said. "I need ten men."

Ben stepped through the gate. Jim wanted to look away but he couldn't. Ben had just put the gun away when several men fought him to the ground. That was the end for Ben now. How could he help his wife and kids from prison?

Jim spent the whole day walking from place to place and looking for work, without luck. Hours later, he returned to the apartment building. His eight-year-old son, Howard, was outside. Jim gave his son a smile. How could a young boy understand that one in four working Americans had no job? An eight-year-old child didn't need to know that.

Suddenly, another child ran up to him. It was Rosy.

"Daddy, Daddy, Daddy!" she cried. "Jay stole!"

Jim carried his daughter to their apartment, where Mae was standing over their oldest son. The ten-year-old's face was red.

Jim put Rosy down. "What's all this about?"

Rosy pointed at the meat on the table. "See?" she said.

There was enough to feed the family for a whole week.

"It's from the butcher shop," said Mae. "He refuses to say a word about it. Don't you, Jay?"

"OK," said Jim to his son. "Pick it up. Let's go."

Jay looked up at his father and the message in his eyes was clear. *Don't make me do this. Can't you see that we need it?*

"Right now!" said Jim.

Then he was out of the building and marching to the butcher shop without another word. His son followed slowly behind, with the stolen food in his hand. At the butcher's, Jay had to give the meat back and apologize. Jim met the butcher's eyes. *I am not bringing up my son to be a thief.*

The butcher nodded. Father and son left the shop. As they walked, Jim was silent, giving his boy time.

At last, Jay spoke. "Marty Johnson had to go and live with his uncle. His parents didn't have enough for them to eat."

Jim turned toward his son. "You were scared," he said. "I understand that. But we don't steal. It doesn't matter what happens. Promise me."

11

Jay managed a nod. "I promise," he said.

"Here's *my* promise." Jim was eye to eye with his son. "We're never going to send you away, son."

The tears came pouring from the little boy's eyes. Jim pulled Jay into his arms and held him as tight as he could.

Chapter 3 An Embarrassment

Mount Vernon, New York, September 23, 1933

The dressing room was a mess. The floor was dirty and the doors were broken. The air smelled of old sweat.

"He's a slow guy," said Joe Gould. "My grandmother could beat him! It'll be an easy fight."

Joe was wearing one of his usual fine brown suits. Jim knew nobody else who hadn't been ruined by the Crash.

The manager was taping up Jim's hands before the fight. He squeezed Jim's right hand, then saw the look of pain on the fighter's face. He played with the hand, examining it carefully.

"This break needs a couple of weeks to get better," he said. "Why didn't you tell me, Jim?"

Jim didn't look up. He had fought in March, although his right hand was still hurt from a fight in January. His opponent was good, and Jim, fighting with a bad hand, had lost in four rounds. But he couldn't stop fighting because he needed the prize money for his family. He fought several more times, hurting his right hand again and again. By now he had to use drugs to control the pain. There was never enough time for it to get better before the next fight.

Joe Gould knew that it wasn't legal to let a boxer fight in this condition. If something went wrong in the ring, it could mean the end for both Joe and Jim.

"I can't get any work," said Jim quietly. "We need the money."

The little manager thought of Mae and the children. "OK," he said. "I'll tape your hand double." Gould knew that double-taping was against the rules, too. "Keep your left hand in his face and, when you can, hit him with a big right. If you finish early, I'll buy you an ice cream!"

He led the boxer past the crowd toward the ring. This crowd was very different from the one at Madison Square Garden years earlier. These people looked poorer and hungrier.

As Jim climbed into the ring, a radio reporter spoke into a microphone. "Just five years ago, Jim Braddock was thought to be ready to fight for the world heavyweight title. But he has lost ten fights in the last year."

The crowd started to shout louder when Abe Feldman walked toward the ring, punching the air.

"Now Braddock fights Feldman," continued the radio man, "a young fighter who has won seventeen times and lost just once."

Jim froze. *This* was the boxer Joe's grandmother could beat?

Feldman was the crowd's favorite. He was young and handsome, like Braddock had been years earlier when he had an unbroken nose and two pretty ears. Braddock's gloves fell to his sides.

Joe pulled Jim's gloves back up. "Jimmy, what are you going to do?"

Jim closed his eyes and everything went away—the crowd's shouts, Mae's worried looks, Ben's gun, Jay's silent tears, all the mistakes of the last four years. He opened his eyes.

"I'm going to get an ice cream!"

♦

Feldman's glove hit Braddock in the face, a hard punch. Jim tried to hit back, but Feldman blocked his punches.

"Come on, Jimmy!" cried Gould from the corner. The manager was sweating almost as much as Braddock, as he jabbed the air and shouted advice. But Braddock could only think about the pain of Feldman's punches. The younger man hit him again and again, but none of Braddock's punches seemed to hit Feldman, who danced around his opponent easily. Suddenly, Feldman threw a combination of punches that threw Braddock back onto the ropes. The crowd began to boo.

"Don't just stand there!" shouted Gould.

Braddock saw an opening in Feldman's defenses and threw a right cross. It hit the fighter's chin and knocked him back. Jim stepped in to finish his opponent, but Feldman put his head down as Braddock threw his big punch. The leather glove hit the top of Feldman's head. There was a sound of bone on bone. The pain in Braddock's right hand was terrible. He held on to Feldman as the bell announced the end of the round. The referee had to send both fighters back to their corners.

Gould quickly took Braddock's right glove off. Even under all the tape, he could see that the hand was really broken.

"I can't let you continue," he said.

Jim thought of the prize money. "I can use my left," he said.

"Don't let Feldman get too close," said Gould, quickly tying the glove back up. "Do what you can with your left."

But Braddock had never had a left-hand punch. Now he couldn't even block with his right, and his feet felt heavy and slow. Punch after punch fell on him.

Time usually slowed down for Jim in the ring, but now it was flying past. He began to throw out his left hand in wild jabs. These missed, but then one punch hit Feldman on the chin and hurt him. Again, the two boxers held on to each other. The crowd began to boo again and shout insults: "Go home!"

Braddock decided that maybe he had one more good right punch in him. He pulled his arm back and threw the punch. It hurt Feldman, but the pain was much worse for Braddock. Under the double tape, his right hand was completely broken. Feldman hit him back, and again Braddock held on to his opponent. He almost fainted from the pain.

The angry boos from the crowd were so loud that he almost didn't hear the bell.

♦

"An embarrassment! That's what it was. An embarrassment!"

Jimmy Johnston, the big fight organizer, was shouting angrily at Joe Gould, who was unusually quiet.

Thirty minutes earlier the referee had ended the fight, announcing that nobody was the winner because Braddock wasn't fit to continue.

"OK, OK, so he's fighting while he's hurt," said Joe. "Maybe your fighters can afford to have a month's rest between fights."

"He almost never hits his opponents any more," answered Johnston. "And now the referee has to stop the fight. A fighter like that keeps the public away. Ticket money will fall." The big man paused. "We're taking away his boxing license. Whatever Braddock was going to do in boxing, he's done it."

When Jim heard the bad news from his manager, he couldn't move, couldn't breathe. The dressing room was small and dirty, so Joe led his boxer back into the hall. The lights threw long shadows on the empty ring. Joe began taping a piece of wood to Jim's broken hand. "Until you get to the hospital."

As he taped the hand, Joe couldn't hold back the memories, all the fights and all the dreams. All the hopes that Jim Braddock would be champion one day. Now those hopes lay as broken as the fighter's hand.

Joe cleared his throat. "Jimmy . . . sometimes you just can't change things. I'm telling you . . . It's finished."

The boxer didn't jump up, shout, or scream. He was quiet for a long time. His face was wet with tears. "Get me one more fight, Joe," said the fighter. "We're down to our last dollar."

15

"I . . . I'm sorry, Jimmy."

After all they had been through together, Joe really was sorry. They had stayed the best of friends through good times and bad. Now it really was the end. Tonight. This was goodbye.

Jim didn't even look up as his manager walked away, leaving him on the seats beside the dark ring. Alone.

Chapter 4   A New Life

"Oh, dear God . . ."

Jim knew that this was the last time he would see this look on Mae's face after a fight. "I don't have the money," he said, too tired to find the words to make it easier. "They refused to pay me, took away my license. They said that I'm finished as a boxer."

The fear in Mae's eyes turned to anger. She didn't care about boxing licenses or fight rules. She only cared about her husband.

"Jimmy, what happened to your hand?"

"It's broken in three places."

Mae wasn't thinking about boxing now. "If you can't work, we won't be able to pay the bills, buy food . . . We'll have to send the children to stay with my sister."

"Mae, I can still work," Jim said. "Get the black shoe polish from the cupboard. Nobody will give me a job if they see this cast on my hand, so we'll cover it up."

Mae saw it in her husband's eyes then—Jim Braddock wasn't going to be beaten. "I'll cut your coat so you can put it on over the cast," she said, opening the shoe polish and spreading it on the white cast. "Now we just need a piece of steak for your face, Jim Braddock!" she laughed.

Six-year-old Rosy's face appeared around the blanket. Jim smiled at her, deciding, not for the first time, that he was a lucky man to have Mae as his wife.

♦

It was early morning and Jim was standing outside the familiar locked gate at Newark docks. As the sun appeared in the east, the foreman, Jake, walked up. Jim put his broken hand behind him. The doctor had said it would be useless for months.

"One, two, three . . ." As usual, Jake walked along the group, pointing to the workers he wanted. ". . . five, six, seven . . ." Jim stood tall. ". . . eight . . ." Jake's eyes fell on Jim, then the foreman pointed at him: "Nine."

A win! Jim stepped forward, knowing that he was one of the lucky few who had work that day.

Minutes later, Jim was meeting his new partner. The young, handsome man introduced himself as Mike Wilson.

"What happened to you?" he asked Jim, staring at the black and blue marks on his face.

"I got into a fight," Jim told the man.

Together the two men had to move a mountain of sacks from one area to another. It took two strong men to lift each sack, using big hooks to pick the sacks up.

Jim found the work very difficult. He had never really used his left hand for anything. It was really hard using the hook with it, while trying to hide the cast on his right hand.

"There was a fighter called Jim Braddock," said Mike. "I listened to his fights on the radio. There's another fighter using the name now, but this guy's no good."

Jim saw the smile on Mike's face. He almost laughed himself, but then the sack fell from the hook in his hand.

Mike saw Jim's cast. "This isn't going to work," he said. "You can't do this job with a bad hand, and you can't slow me down. I need this job."

Jim gave his partner a quick look. "Listen, I can do this."

Suddenly, a new voice shouted, "What's happening here?" It was the foreman, and he was staring at Jim's bad hand.

Instead of trying to explain, Jim sank the hook back into the sack with his left hand. Then he waited, unable to do anything until his partner moved. After a few terrible seconds, Mike sunk the hook into his end of the sack. The two men lifted the heavy sack together and carried it across the dock. Then they moved for another sack, then another, and another.

Jake, the foreman, stood there with arms crossed, watching every move. Finally, he walked away.

Jim lifted his face to Mike. "Thanks," he said.

♦

It was raining hard, but Mae didn't move. Her place in this soup line was too valuable. Hundreds of people were ahead of her, but a lot were behind her, too. They were all waiting for free soup and bread from the truck at the head of the line. Mae held Rosy in her arms. The two boys ran around playing.

"You need to stand for a few minutes, Rosy," said Mae.

"I don't want to!" cried Rosy. "The sidewalk's wet!"

"Who's making all this noise?"

Immediately, Rosy's crying stopped. Her father appeared beside her, big and strong and with a smile on his face for her.

As he lifted Rosy, Jim told Mae, "I got a job at the docks."

Mae noticed something inside Jim's coat. His boxing shoes. She wasn't surprised to see them. A few boxing organizers in expensive suits couldn't stop her husband from fighting, even if they had taken away his license.

"Are you training today?" she asked him.

"I was thinking of selling them," said Jim. "Then we can pay the grocer by the end of the week."

Mae didn't know what to say. At last she said, "Don't take less than a dollar, Jim."

He saw the tears in her eyes. "Go home. I'll stand in line."

She handed him the empty pot and took the children home. Jim's eyes followed them, and then he looked forward again, turning his collar up against the wind. The soup truck seemed far, far away, but Jim had become good at waiting.

Hours later, familiar sounds greeted Jim's ears—jump ropes hitting the wooden floors, leather gloves hitting punching bags. This was the gym that Jim had trained in for years. It was the place where he had first met Joe Gould. Even now, part of him wanted to get into the ring and fight.

As he entered the gym, the usual smell of leather and sweat hit him. He looked at all the boxers training hard.

"Jimmy!" said a friendly voice. "Have you come to train?"

It was Joe Jeannette, the owner of the gym. The old fighter had never been a champion, but he had always been a hero to Jim. A great boxer with quick hands and a knockout punch, Jeannette had been one of the best heavyweights in the country. But he was a black man, and few white boxers agreed to fight him. Jeannette never had the chance to fight for the title. But Jeannette couldn't stay away from the fight game. He had become a referee, and he had opened this gym. He was never too busy to give advice to a young boxer.

Jim tried to return Jeannette's smile, but he couldn't. He put the soup pot down and pulled his boxing shoes out of his coat.

A few minutes later, Joe Gould stepped onto the gym floor. He was here to see a new boxer, not Jim Braddock. Joe watched as Jim handed his boxing shoes to a young, black boxer, who paid Jim ten cents. Then Jim picked up his soup and bread and turned toward the front entrance.

Joe Jeannette looked up and saw the manager standing at the back of the gym. His eyes held a question for Joe, but Joe just shook his head and stepped behind the door.

It's better for both of us if Jim doesn't see me, Joe thought.

19

Chapter 5   Broken Promises

Jim sat at the kitchen table reading out President Franklin Delano Roosevelt's speech from the newspaper. He tried to find hope in the President's words. According to Roosevelt, there was only one thing for Americans to fear—"fear itself." Mae counted out coins from the rainy-day jar.

Jim's week had become an unending string of gray mornings and sweaty afternoons of hard work at the docks. Jim and Mike worked together every day, and Jim did all the work with his left hand. In the evenings, he had another job—more long, hard work with only his left hand. Mae was usually asleep on the sofa by the time Jim got home at night.

That night she was woken by the sound of coins dropping into the jar. She saw her husband walk toward their bed.

Jim looked down at the clean, white sheets. He wanted nothing more than to fall into them, but then he looked down at his own dirty, sweaty body, and lay down on the floor.

"Jimmy," Mae whispered. "We can wash the sheets."

But Jim was already asleep. Mae pulled the covers off the bed and lay down on the floor, beside her husband.

♦

The winter of 1933–34 was one of the coldest in recent memory. One morning, Mae and Rosy walked with the boys to school. They were walking back down the snowy street when Mae saw a shiny new car outside their building.

"Mommy, who's the man at our house?" asked Rosy.

Mae walked up to the man, whose uniform showed that he was the gas and electricity man. "Can I help you, sir?"

"I'm sorry, ma'am. You haven't paid the bills, and I have to cut your electricity off."

The man was in his thirties, but his eyes looked older.

"You can't," said Mae. "We have kids. *Please.*"

"If I don't, I'll lose my job," said the man sadly.

Work at the docks finished early that day. Jim and his work partner Mike started walking around local towns, looking for work. There was none anywhere that day. Tired and cold, they started for home.

"We have until tomorrow," cried a loud voice.

Jim's steps slowed. Across the street, a young man was arguing with two city police officers. His wife stood beside him, fighting back tears. The couple's furniture was on the sidewalk all around them. The officers were moving them from their apartment.

The two officers wore fine, new uniforms. The younger of the two was polite. The older man had heard every excuse before, and he was tired of listening.

Jim watched as the young husband tried to pull a piece of paper out of the officer's hand.

"This says we have another day," he cried.

"Come on," said Mike, pulling Jim's arm. But Jim was already moving across the street and Mike went with him.

"You can't do this," the young woman was saying. "We'll never get back in."

Her husband jumped in front of the officers as they moved to fit a new lock to the building's front door. "Please, I'm starting a factory job next week . . ."

The officers pushed him away and put the lock on.

"Excuse me," said Mike politely, then louder: "Excuse me!" The officers stared at him. "Please can I have a look at that notice? The law says that I'm allowed to." He stepped forward. "Let me just have a look at the date on it. If everything's OK with it, we'll just walk away."

"Or else what?" demanded the younger officer. The older officer was looking at Jim.

Mike smiled. "You guys know Jim Braddock, don't you?"

The older officer's attitude changed immediately. "I've seen you fight, Jim," he said.

Mike looked down at the document in the older man's hand. "What do you say, guys? Mistakes happen all the time."

The officer nodded. "Maybe we got our days mixed up," he said, removing the lock from the door.

As the two officers walked away, Mike and Jim began to help the couple move their furniture back inside.

"So you're a lawyer?" asked Jim.

Mike shook his head. "A banker, but I hired enough lawyers to have a good idea of the law. It doesn't matter now . . . I lost it all in '29." He looked Jim in the eyes. "You know, there are people living in Central Park. The government has failed us. We need to organize. Fight back."

Jim shook his head. "Fight what? Bad luck? You have to trust that the government will solve things in the end. I like what President Roosevelt says."

"Forget Roosevelt!" shouted Mike. "He hasn't given me my house back yet!"

Jim looked in surprise at the terrible anger in his friend's eyes.

♦

The blanket didn't hang in the middle of the room. Now the three children had it around them, as they lay in bed. Jim could see their breath in the cold air. Every piece of clothing in the apartment was piled on top of them.

He crossed the room and threw a piece of a wooden sign onto the fire in the stove. Mae emptied the rainy-day jar onto the table. She began to push the coins around.

"Six dollars and seventy cents," said Jim, joining his wife. "How much would it cost to turn the electricity back on?"

"Thirty-three dollars and ten cents," whispered Mae.

"If I work twenty-six hours out of every twenty-four, it still won't be enough." Jim seemed suddenly weaker. He looked at Mae. "Think of all the other guys who wanted to marry you."

"What happened to those guys?" joked Mae, then she squeezed his hand. "I married the guy I love."

A wet cough from across the room interrupted them. "It's Howard," said Mae sadly. "He's been sick since this afternoon."

When Mae woke up the next morning, Jim had already gone out into the terrible cold. She spent the morning trying to keep the children warm, burning pieces of wood they had taken from signs in the street. Howard lay close to the stove, his face red with fever. Fighting back the tears, his mother held a glass of water to his lips. The boy was getting sicker.

Not wanting her children to see her cry, Mae rushed out the door and stood in the snow. Bitter tears ran down her face.

She cared only about keeping this family together. Jim was killing himself trying to do this, but it wasn't working. Now they had lost their heat and electric power. Mae knew what she had to do. She rushed inside to dress her children warmly for the trip across the river to New York City.

♦

As Jim stepped through the door, the apartment was as cold as the air outside. He met silence. No little bodies ran to him with open arms. By the stove, Mae sat alone, staring into the dying flames. She couldn't meet his eyes.

"Howard was getting worse," she explained. "Then Rosy started to get sick."

"Where are they, Mae?"

"The boys are at my father's house. Rosy's going to stay with my sister. We can't keep them warm, Jim."

Jim's emotions were almost too strong for words—fear, sadness, anger. He pointed a finger at Mae. "You don't decide what happens to our children without me."

Mae stood and held his arms. "Jimmy, if they get really sick, we don't have the money for a doctor."

"If you send them away, this has all been for nothing," he said angrily. "It means that we lost." He shook Mae's arms off. "I made a promise to Jay, do you understand? I promised that we would never send him away."

Without another word, he turned and walked across the freezing room and out of the door.

Later that afternoon, he stood at the wooden counter of the Newark relief office. An unsmiling woman counted out twelve dollars and eighty cents, which she placed in a white envelope. Jim's hand shook as he signed for the money, trying not to blame himself for what he had done. Ashamed, he put the envelope into his pocket.

He pushed his way through the unhappy crowd. They were lawyers and dock workers, teachers and factory workers. Bankers and builders. Now, unable to earn money themselves, they were here to receive money from the state. Some were so ashamed that, like Jim, they looked only at the floor. Others looked straight ahead with empty stares.

After Jim crossed the river to Manhattan, he walked past all the homeless people in the city who seemed to have no hope. The story was the same everywhere: *No work. No money.*

At last, Jim reached the streets around Madison Square Garden. There were no bright lights now, no people in expensive clothes waiting outside. Instead, homeless people searched for anything they could use.

Jim went to the familiar side door. The sign for the next fight showed two boxers standing with gloves up. Jim remembered when his picture had been on signs like this. He remembered the fight with Tuffy Griffiths, the dream of that night when the future looked bright for Jim Braddock.

But then another, less happy memory came to mind—the fight

against Tommy Loughran. It was July 1929—just four months before the Crash. Jim was fighting for the title of light heavyweight champion, but it was the fight that turned Braddock into a boxer of "failed promise."

The New York crowd had wanted Braddock to win, and the fight had started well, too. But things changed in the second round. Loughran began to dance around the ring, dodging Braddock's punches easily. He had discovered Braddock's biggest weakness—no left-hand punch.

In the rest of the fight, Braddock had hit the champion with a few good punches, but it wasn't enough. The judges all decided that Loughran was the winner. The newspapers weren't kind to Braddock, who had looked slow in the last three rounds. His dream of winning the title seemed to be at an end.

Now, years later, Jim stood in the shadows in Madison Square Garden and said the same words that he had said after the Loughran fight: "I don't know what went wrong."

He opened the side door and started up the stairs. The climb to the Madison Square Garden boxing club was the hardest of his life. The club was a place where the rich money-makers of New York's boxing world could relax and do business. It wasn't high above street level, but it was like another world.

At first, nobody noticed as Jim Braddock walked into the smoky room. He went up to two men in the center of the room.

"Mr. Allen . . . Phil . . ."

The men looked up at the fighter. Others noticed and conversations around the room died. Jim cleared his throat.

"I'm here because we can't afford to pay the heating bills. We had to send our kids away . . . I just need enough money to get my children back." Jim took off his hat and stretched it out.

The whole room was silent now. Mr. Allen put his hand in his pocket. "Sure, Jim." He placed a few coins into Jim's hat.

"Thank you," replied Jim. Then he offered his hat to the others around the room. Everybody gave some money—even Jimmy Johnston, the man who had taken away Jim's license.

Finally, Jim stopped in front of Joe Gould. "I'm sorry, Joe," he told his old manager.

"What do you have to be sorry about, Jim?" said Joe. "How much more do you need?"

"One dollar and fifty cents, I think," whispered Jim. Joe placed the exact amount in Jim's hat.

When Jim left the club, it was dark outside and streetlights lit the icy sidewalks. Jim walked past a store that had gone out of business. His face looked back at him from the dark glass of the store window. He had seen that look before. It was on the face of the man in his old suit selling apples on the street corner. It was on the face of the banker waiting in line for hours at the Newark relief office.

Jim had never understood how a proud man could sink so low. Now, with the money in his pocket to get his children back, Jim knew. He finally understood.

◆

The next night, Mae opened the apartment door and turned on the electric light. Jay and Howard ran inside, followed by Jim, who was carrying the sleeping Rosy.

Jim was happy to see his family together and home again, but he felt other emotions, too. He knew now how easily their world could be destroyed.

He couldn't sleep that night. When the sun finally appeared, he got up and dressed silently. Before he left for another long day of work, he stood at the door and looked at his family. A boxer entered the ring alone. If he was knocked down, he alone could stand up and continue fighting. Jim was alone now, as he left the house and went looking for work.

Chapter 6   One Fight Only

Spring had come to Newark at last, and the Braddock family had joined other families at the local church. Once a month the priest, Father Rorick, organized a birthday party for all the children whose parents couldn't afford a party.

Jim and Mae watched as their children joined all the others around a large wooden table with two big cakes. Everybody starting singing, "Happy birthday to you . . . Happy birthday to you . . ."

Jim put his hand around Mae, happy that the cast was off at last. When it was time to sing the names, the different families all sang a different name.

"Happy birthday, dear Jay," sang the Braddocks. "Happy birthday to you!"

Howard pulled his father's arm. "It was better when we had our own cake," he said.

Father Rorick heard him. "Do you know I boxed your father a long time ago?"

Howard couldn't believe it. He looked at his father in surprise. "You hit Father Rorick?"

"As often as possible," said Jim with a big smile.

Mae Braddock joined the two men. She looked worried. "Jimmy . . ." She looked across the road. Mike, Jim's work partner at the docks, was sitting at the end of a long table. His wife, Sara, held their baby daughter in her arms and she was shouting at Mike.

"You're always trying to fix the world!" she shouted. "Why don't you fix your own family? What kind of father are you? Too proud to let people know that our daughter can't have her own birthday cake . . ."

Mike stared back angrily. "Are you joking, Sara?"

Everybody watched the argument. Even the children at the party stopped playing.

Jim walked over and separated the angry couple. "Hey, where's the referee?" he asked.

"This is between husband and wife, Jim," Mike said angrily.

"How can you call yourself that?" cried Sara.

Mike jumped up angrily, and Jim stopped him with a strong hand in the middle of his chest.

"Calm down, Mike," he said. "Have a rest."

But Mike couldn't calm down now. He pushed Jim.

"There's no need for this," said the boxer.

"Jim Braddock, big fighter . . ." said Mike, and he threw a punch at his work partner.

Jim knocked it away and then held Mike's arm. "Mike, I don't want to fight you," he said.

"You couldn't do it in the ring . . ." said Mike angrily.

He rushed at Jim again. Jim pushed him to the side and Mike fell, hitting his head on the sidewalk.

"Jim, no!" screamed Sara.

As Mike got to his feet, blood ran down his face. Sara went up to him, still holding their baby. Mike pushed her away.

"Leave me alone," he said to her and Jim. He turned and ran down the street.

When he had gone, Sara turned to Jim. Tears poured down her face as she cried, "He wasn't going to hit me, Jim!"

Sara began to chase her husband down the street. Jim looked up at Mae, who had tears in her eyes, too.

"Why was it so hard just to come over for cake?" she asked.

"Maybe he just needed a little time," said Jim angrily. "It's not always easy . . . Maybe he just needed a little time!"

Mae shook her finger at him. "Not at me, James Braddock!" she cried. "Do you hear? I know it's hard. But don't get mad at me!"

♦

Jim returned from work one afternoon and found his children playing in front of the apartment building.

Rosy looked up at him. "Teach me how to fight," she said.

"I can't," said Jim. "I'll get in trouble with Mommy."

Rosy just looked at her father with the same stare that Mae had. Jim couldn't say no to that look.

"OK," he said. "It's all about how you hold your body. Put your right hand here and your left here . . ." Jim positioned her until she was standing like a little boxer. Then she threw a punch, which Jim caught in his big hand.

"Look at that!" he cried. "You have a better jab than I did!"

As he and Rosy laughed, a familiar car stopped outside the building.

"You're a brave man," called Joe Gould.

Jim smiled. "Not really. Mae's at the store."

Rosy, who wasn't yet finished with her boxing lesson, threw another punch. It hit Jim right on the chin.

"OK, Rosy," he said. "Good punch. Now go and box shadows while I talk to Uncle Joe."

Jim looked at the manager's fine, new suit. "Still looking fashionable, I see," he said.

"You have to show you're doing well," answered Joe. He gave Jim a friendly punch on the arm. "Good to see you, Jimmy." Then: "I've got you a fight."

Jim wasn't sure. "What about my boxing license?"

"The organizers will let you fight one time only," said Joe.

Jim asked the most important question: "How much?"

"Two hundred and fifty dollars," Joe replied. "You're on the big show at the Madison Square Garden Bowl in Long Island City . . ." He paused. ". . . tomorrow night."

Jim turned and walked away. He couldn't believe that his old friend and partner would play a joke like this on him.

Joe chased after him. "You fight Corn Griffin, Jimmy . . . the number two heavyweight in the world. He needs a fight before he boxes for the title."

Jim's eyes were dangerous. "Joe, this isn't funny."

"No one's trying to be kind to you. Griffin's opponent got cut and can't fight. They needed someone they could throw in the ring immediately. Nobody will take a fight against Griffin without training, so . . ." Joe looked away. "I . . . told them that Griffin could knock out a guy who has never been knocked out before . . . You're meat, Jimmy . . . They just need somebody to stand in that ring and be knocked out."

Finally, Jim smiled and put a hand on Joe's shoulder. Then he looked his manager in the eye. "Joe. For two hundred and fifty dollars, I'd fight your wife."

When Mae got home later, she wasn't happy about the news. Jim talked more—about how it was only one fight, about how long he would have to work at the docks for so much money.

In the end, Mae told Jim to take the fight. But that night she sat on the sofa in the dark and watched her sleeping husband through eyes red from crying.

♦

The next morning, the three children were outside early, but they didn't go out to play. They walked to the local butcher shop. Rosy knocked on the window.

Sam, the butcher, looked down at the three children. "We're closed today." His eye fell on Jay, remembering the time when the boy had stolen from his shop. "Well, look who's here. Shall I lock everything up?"

Jay's face was red, but he bravely stood by his sister, who walked up to the counter.

"I need a piece of meat, please, sir," she said. "Steak."

"Do you have any money?"

Rosy shook her head and the look in Sam's eyes became softer. "I can't just give the meat away."

"It's not for me . . . It's for my dad," Rosy replied. "He needs it to win a boxing fight."

Chapter 7   Back in the Ring

Long Island City, New York, June 14, 1934

Jim's name wasn't even on the sign, but he didn't care. Two hundred and fifty dollars and the chance to punch something real were the only things on his mind.

Joe Gould didn't know what to think about the fight. The manager had tried to get Braddock back in the ring since the time Jim had walked around the boxing club with his hat in his hand. Joe had pushed his way into Jimmy Johnston's office again and again, trying to get Jim a fight.

He had been outside Johnston's office when the fight organizer got the bad news about Griffin's opponent, just two days before the big fight. This left Johnston with a problem. Griffin was a promising young star in the boxing world, and Johnston wanted to get the New York sports world interested in him. The young Southern boxer needed to beat a fighter in the city who had once been a big name. Now it seemed that Jim Braddock was the right choice—especially as Braddock's manager was waiting outside Johnston's office.

Joe had accepted the offer, but now, on fight night, he was worried. He knew that Jim hadn't fought in over a year. Except for today, he hadn't trained in a long time. He had even sold his boxing gloves and shoes. Joe had to borrow some so that his boxer could fight.

As the manager bent to tie up his boxing shoes, Jim smiled. "We both know what this is, Joe. It's a chance for me to earn some money for my family. And it's a chance to say goodbye to boxing in a big fight in front of a big crowd."

Suddenly, there was a loud noise from Jim's stomach.

"What was that?" cried Joe.

"We got to the soup line too late this morning," said Jim. "The food was all gone."

Joe jumped to his feet. "How are you going to fight with an empty stomach?" he shouted. He ran from the room and appeared a few minutes later with a bowl of thick meat soup in his hand. "Eat fast," he said.

"Where's the spoon?" asked Jim. He began to put one hand into the bowl.

"Stop!" cried Joe. "I don't have time to tape your hands again. I'll find a spoon!"

Joe rushed out again, but Jim couldn't wait. He pushed his face into the bowl and began eating. He didn't notice the changing room door opening.

"I don't believe it! Am I seeing a ghost?" said a voice. Jim looked up, with food on his chin. A young man at the door was giving Jim an unpleasant smile. "Isn't that James J. Braddock? When I saw the name, I thought it *must* be a different guy." The man stepped into the room and took out a reporter's notebook. "How's your right hand now, Jim?"

Jim's eyes narrowed as he recognized the reporter. He said the man's name: "Sporty Lewis."

Jim remembered what Lewis had written about his fight with Tommy Loughran. He repeated the reporter's words to himself: "Loughran destroyed the unskilled New Jersey fighter. The fight was a funeral with the body still breathing."

Lewis saw the look in Jim's eyes and stopped smiling. "I don't fight the fights, Braddock. I just write about them."

Jim stepped up to Sporty, toe to toe and eye to eye. "Save that garbage for your readers," he said.

Suddenly, the door opened and an official pointed at Jim. "It's time," he said.

Jim left the room, keeping his eyes on Sporty Lewis's. Sporty stared after him, pale and shaken.

"That guy," he said to the official. "What a loser!"

Minutes later, Sporty was back in his seat by the side of the boxing ring. A young reporter next to him asked, "Who's Jim Braddock?"

"Get your pencil out, kid," Sporty Lewis said. "I have your story for you: 'The walk from the changing room to the ring was the only time tonight that Jim Braddock was seen on his feet.'"

♦

"In this corner, Corn Griffin!"

Griffin jumped to the center of the ring and lifted his thick arms above his head. The tall young boxer wore a confident smile on his face. He was young and powerful, a natural heavyweight with long arms and a big punch.

"And in this corner . . . from New Jersey . . . Jim Braddock!"

The crowd were silent.

When the bell rang, Griffin came out punching hard and fast. Braddock danced and dodged, doing everything possible to keep away from Corn's powerful punches. After thirty seconds, Braddock decided that this fight was a bad idea. His opponent had trained hard and was ready to fight. He timed his jabs and punches to Braddock's body perfectly. Jim's only goal now was to finish the fight without getting hurt. He had to be able to work at the docks the next day.

Suddenly, a big left-hand punch from Griffin hit Braddock on the side of the head. He went down. As he lay there, the clocks seemed to stop.

"Braddock's down!" cried the announcer over the crowd's boos.

"One . . . two . . . three . . ." counted the referee. Braddock tried to get to his feet. "Four . . . five . . . six . . ."

Braddock was on one knee, but the referee continued counting.

"Get up and use your left!" Gould called to his fighter.

Finally, Braddock stood. The referee walked over to him and checked his eyes and the cut in his mouth.

"It's finished, Braddock," he said.

Braddock looked across the ring at his opponent and joked, "He doesn't look so bad." But the referee began to lift his hand to end the fight. Jim held his arm with two gloved hands. "Please. Let me fight."

The referee paused, looking hard at Jim, and then he stepped to the side. The fight could continue!

Griffin was waiting to continue his attack. Braddock answered one punch with a left-hand jab. It didn't hurt Griffin, but Jim was surprised that he could throw a left-hand punch at all.

In the second round, Griffin continued to chase Braddock around the ring. The young fighter wanted to win by a knockout, and Jim had to keep moving to dodge Corn's punches.

At the end of the round, Jim sat heavily in his corner. Joe poured water in the fighter's mouth. When it ran out again into the waiting bucket, it was pink with blood. Jim hardly heard his manager's words, though they were screamed into his face.

"He's half a step behind you!" shouted Joe. "Move to the side and see what happens. Hit him with two jabs and then the big punch."

The bell rang for the third round. Braddock moved out of his corner slowly; Griffin came out punching. Remembering Gould's advice, Braddock moved his shoulders to one side. Griffin didn't see the move and Braddock hit him with a right that sent Griffin to the floor. The referee started counting.

"That's it!" screamed Gould. The little manager started to dance and throw punches in the air.

"Three . . ." The referee's count continued.

Joe's eyes, shining with happiness and surprise, met Jim's. "Where have you been, Jimmy Braddock?"

Griffin was back on his feet, but now Jim was the one moving with confidence. Braddock rushed forward, throwing punch after punch.

Gould was screaming. "That's it! Send him home. Send him back South or wherever he comes from!"

The punches didn't stop. They fell like rain on the soup line, like snow on the Newark docks. Finally, Braddock delivered a hard right punch and stepped away. The crowd just watched as Griffin fell forward. He landed on the floor and stayed there.

In the silence that followed, Jim saw Sporty Lewis next to the ring. The reporter's eyes were big with surprise. The next second, the crowd went wild.

"I can't believe it!" the radio announcer was saying. "Corn Griffin, the number two challenger for the heavyweight title, has been knocked out by Jim Braddock in the third round!"

♦

Before he left the dressing room with Joe Gould, Jim finished the bowl of food.

"Imagine what I could do if I had steak," he joked.

On their way out, they paused to watch the end of the evening's main event. The heavyweight champion of the world, Primo Carnera, was defending his title against a strong, young boxer called Max Baer. Baer's punch was so powerful that he had once killed a man in the ring. This was the fight the crowd had really come to see.

In the last round of the fight, Max Baer's powerful punches were falling on Carnera without end. Carnera fell to the floor.

"Imagine a punch like that hitting you," Joe said.

Carnera was an enormous man, but Baer was much faster. All night he had danced and dodged Carnera's fists. Now, Carnera was bloody and beaten as he got to his feet, holding the rope with one glove. Baer just laughed at the defending champion, knocking away his weak punches easily.

"Primo Carnera has been knocked down eleven times!" the radio announcer was saying. "And Max Baer looks sure that he will be the next champion!"

Carnera moved his tired body toward his opponent for a final attack. The challenger waited patiently with an ugly smile on his handsome face. When Carnera reached the center of the ring, Baer decided to end the fight, throwing punch after punch at the champion. It was so terrible that even Joe couldn't watch.

Chapter 8   A Second Chance

Jim stepped out of the car in front of his apartment house.

"Are you sure you won't come in and say hello?" he asked.

"Are you still married to the same girl?" asked Joe.

Jim gave the usual answer. "I was the last time I looked."

Joe smiled. "Good night, Jimmy."

The car drove off, and Jim stood outside the building. The Braddocks had sold their radio, so Mae and the kids didn't know the result of tonight's fight.

The door opened and Jay, Howard, and Rosy looked up at him with hopeful faces. Mae stood silently.

"I won," he said.

The children screamed and rushed toward him. Rosy pulled on his arm. "Daddy, Daddy, you have to see what I got you!" She ran to the ice box. "Put it on your eyes," she said, pushing a thick steak into her father's hands.

Jim looked at the meat. "Where did you get this?"

"They all went to the butcher shop," said Mae. "I tried to take it back, but the butcher says he *gave* it to her."

"It's a steak," said Rosy. "It'll fix your face."

Jim held the thick steak up. He could almost smell it, hear it cooking. He went down on his knees to speak to his daughter—fighter to fighter. "Rosy, we have to eat this."

But Rosy shouted, "No! You have to put it on your face."

Jim knew that it was useless to argue. He lay back and placed the cool steak across his eyes. He waited a few seconds, and then lifted one edge of the meat.

Jay turned to his mother. "Do the announcer's voice, Mom."

"Come on, Mae," said Jim with a smile. "Do the announcer."

Mae's voice became loud. "Introducing the holder of the amateur title for light heavyweight and heavyweight . . . from New Jersey . . . the future heavyweight champion of the world . . . James J. Braddock."

These last words were shouted. The kids went wild, laughing and jumping around the room. Jim took the steak from his face.

"This really worked," he told his daughter. "Let's eat!"

He crossed to the stove and started cooking the meat. Soon the sound and the delicious smell filled the apartment.

"Jim," Mae whispered. "Is it really just one fight, or are they letting you back in?"

Jim kissed her head. "It was just the one fight."

Relief swept through Mae. As she went to the stove to get the steak, she said silent thanks that her husband would never step inside the ring again.

♦

The early morning walk to the docks was the same as usual, but Jim felt different. His body ached, but his steps were quicker than they had been in months.

He joined the group of men at the fence. Finally, the foreman Jake appeared and began pointing to men.

"Six, seven, eight . . ." Jake's eyes passed Jim, then returned to him. The foreman said Jim's name and everybody turned to look. "Nine."

Jim closed his eyes in relief. As he passed through the gate, Jake said to him, "I listened to the fight last night." He took out his newspaper. Jim's eyes ran over the words:

BRADDOCK KNOCKOUT OVER GRIFFIN IN 3

Jim shook his head, not believing it. A few men crowded round to hear what he had to say. They seemed surprised that he had come to work today.

"It was one night only," explained Jim. "My share was a hundred and twenty five dollars. We had bills of one hundred and twenty to pay. That left me with five dollars."

Jake laughed. "That makes you a rich man." Then he said seriously, "Good fight."

Jim could see that these men around him, with their old clothes and tired faces, had found hope watching him fight. He had fought something real, something he could see—they all wished for that chance.

He joined his partner, Mike. Words weren't necessary. The two picked up their hooks and began to work, moving the heavy sacks.

"Why didn't you tell me you were going to win again?" said Mike. "I didn't put any money on you."

Mike smiled, but it wasn't the smile Jim remembered. It was tired. Less happy.

"Come on," Mike said. "Talk me through that last round."

Jim started describing the events of the last round again. Since the cast had come off his arm, he worked with both hands. Without thinking, he moved the hook to his left hand and continued working with smooth, strong movements.

◆

A week later, Mae was walking back from the stores with Rosy when she saw a shiny new car drive away from their apartment house. Joe Gould's car.

She found Jim standing in the yard behind the building. He looked so happy, so handsome and confident in the sun, with his square chin and his bright eyes up to the blue sky. Then he turned and Mae felt her heart stop. She saw it in his eyes—the old excitement.

"Joe was here," said Jim. "He thinks they'll let me box again."

It was hard for Mae to speak. "You said it was one fight."

"It's my chance, Mae, to make you and the kids proud."

Mae fought to control her fear and anger. "I *am* proud . . . and grateful. But what would we do if something bad happened to you? Something worse than a broken hand, so you couldn't work?"

She couldn't even tell her worst fear: *What will happen if you're killed?*

"What would happen to us?" demanded Mae. "To the children? We're hardly managing now."

Jim shook his head sadly. He waved a hand at the broken building, the empty yard. Couldn't she see? He was already killing himself—and for what? A few coins at the end of a long day's work? "I have to do better than I'm doing," he replied.

Mae stepped closer. "Things are better now. Please, Jim . . ."

He wanted to take her in his arms, but he stopped himself. He had to think about the family's future. The strength was clear in his voice. "I can still take a few punches. At least in the ring you know who's hitting you."

Mae felt helpless as she watched him walk to the building's dark back door. *This isn't over, James Braddock,* she promised.

◆

The next morning Jim left early for the gym. Mae left the apartment house, too. She took the kids to her sister's house, and then she crossed the Hudson River to New York City.

She was going to the small part of the city known as the Upper East Side. It was an area of beautiful houses, expensive apartment buildings, and fine hotels. Some of the richest people in the country lived on the blocks along the city's Central Park.

Two streets away, the buildings weren't quite so beautiful, but they were still home to wealthy people. In front of each apartment building, a uniformed doorman stood guard.

When she reached the tall building, she looked up, trying to guess how many floors it had. She went through the beautiful entrance hall to the elevator. On the fifteenth floor, she moved down the line of doors.

She knocked on one and called politely, "Open the door, Joe." There was no answer. She tried again, and again, but nobody came to the door. "Joe, open this door now!" Mae shouted. "You're not going to hide in your expensive apartment while you turn my husband into a punching bag. I won't let you get him hurt again!"

The door opened. "You'd better come in," said Joe Gould.

As she pushed past him, Mae's anger died. She had expected the manager's home to be beautiful. But she looked around now at a completely empty apartment.

Minutes later, she sat on a camping chair, drinking tea with Joe and his wife Lucille. She hadn't expected this friendly welcome.

"Sorry," said Joe, pointing to the door. "People have to think you're doing well."

"I thought . . ." said Mae.

"That's the plan," said Joe, touching his fine brown suit. "Show people you're doing well, even if you're not. We sold the last of the furniture last week," he continued, "so Jimmy could train."

"Why?" Mae asked.

"Sometimes you see something in a fighter, something to hope for," answered Joe. "Jimmy's what I hope for."

Mae shook her head. "This is crazy. You don't even know if you can get him a fight, do you?"

"I'll get him a fight," Joe said, "if it's the last thing I do."

Chapter 9   Not the Same Guy

The gym owner, Joe Jeannette, looked pleased. "You've been training, Jimmy."

"I've been working, Joe. Not training."

"Show me what work you did."

"I was lifting sacks at the dock," explained Jim. "We used a hook, like this." He showed the movement.

"That's the perfect punching exercise," said Jeannette. "You've been getting a powerful left hand, and you didn't even know it."

In the next few weeks, Braddock trained hard. After all those months of hard work, it was like a vacation to train with Jeannette. But the trainer pushed him hard. Every week there were new exercises, new skills to learn and practice.

While Braddock worked at the gym, Joe Gould was busy in other ways. At Madison Square Garden, he walked into Jimmy Johnston's office and sat down.

"You're going to arrange a fight between Jim Braddock and John Henry Lewis."

Johnston looked up from the papers he was signing. "Now why would I do that?"

Joe smiled confidently. "Lewis is number two in line to fight for the heavyweight title, and he's already beaten Braddock once before. So put Braddock against Lewis. If Lewis wins, your boy has had a good practice fight before his next opponent, and you make some money. If, by some chance, Braddock beats Lewis, you have a people's favorite, which means you make *more* money. Whatever happens, you're richer with Braddock back in the ring." Gould sat back. "So what do you say?"

As soon as he got an answer, Joe rushed back to the gym.

"I got you a fight," he told Jim from the ropes. "You're going to fight John Henry Lewis again."

Jim climbed out of the ring. "I could kiss you."

Joe took a step back. "Please don't!" The manager became suddenly serious. "I won't lie, Jimmy. You're in this fight because you're meat. But if you win it, I can get you another one. If you win the next, then everything changes."

Jim understood. He turned toward the heavy punching bag.

"Jimmy," Joe called.

Jim turned and saw the old fire in his manager's eyes.

"Win!" said Joe.

♦

It was the afternoon before the fight. Jim was still at home.

"I know this isn't what you wanted," he said softly to Mae. "But I can't win if you don't support me."

Mae put the pile of clean clothes down and stepped up to her husband. "I always support you," she whispered.

While their parents were kissing, the three children took their chance to run out of the apartment. They walked through the small crowd that stood outside the building. Soon they stood again in the butcher shop.

"What can I do for you today?" Sam, the butcher, asked.

"My dad's fighting a man who beat him badly once before," said Rosy anxiously. "What kind of steaks do you have?"

Down the block, Jim stepped out of the apartment house and was met by a small crowd of neighbors.

"We're all supporting you," said an old man.

"Take him down, Jim!" cried another.

Suddenly, a familiar face appeared in front of Jim—Mike Wilson. They shook hands.

"I put some money on you," Mike said.

"Mike, everybody expects Lewis to win," said Jim.

But Mike just gave a confident smile. "Do you need some help in your corner?" he asked.

Jim shook his head. "I have my regular guys for that. You know how it is, Mike."

Mike's shoulders dropped, but he tried to laugh. "Sure I do, Jim. Now go and win the fight!"

♦

The powerful jab pushed Braddock back against the ropes. John Henry Lewis was a young black boxer with quick hands and a lot of skill. His perfectly timed combinations of punches pushed Jim on to the ropes again.

"Lewis is here to repeat his win over Braddock," said the radio announcer.

For three rounds, the two fighters danced around the ring, looking for the other man's weak areas. Then, in the fourth round, the fight became serious. The fighters went toe to toe, refusing to step back.

In his corner at the end of the round, Lewis looked confused.

"You beat this guy easily last time!" his manager screamed.

Lewis just shook his head. "He isn't the same guy."

In the opposite corner, Gould checked Braddock's face. The boxer was tired and breathing hard, his body covered with sweat.

"He's even faster than I remember," said Jim.

Gould spoke into the boxer's ear. "He's fast, but he'll be slower after a few more punches. Watch him—he always moves to the right."

Both fighters started round five like mad animals. Leather gloves flew, and neither man backed away. Suddenly, Braddock hit his opponent with a powerful cross and Lewis was down on one knee. When the fight continued, Lewis wasn't able to protect himself, letting Braddock knock him back on to the ropes.

In the end, the judges gave the fight to Braddock. Some sports reporters said that he had deserved to win. Others said that he had just hit Lewis with a few lucky punches.

As Joe Gould gave Jim his share of the prize money, he said, "Take care of yourself. Our luck has changed—I'm sure of it."

♦

A month later, in December 1934, Jimmy Johnston made the announcement that Joe Gould expected. He was going to organize fights among the top heavyweight boxers. Finally, one man would be chosen to fight the champion, Max Baer, for the heavyweight title. Johnston had several boxers in mind, but Braddock wasn't one of them. He didn't think that Braddock was lucky—he was *good*. Johnston didn't want the New Jersey boxer to stop another of his young stars.

But Gould refused to take no for an answer. Again and again he went to Johnston's office, trying to get a fight for his man.

"How about a fight with Art Lasky?" he tried.

At first Johnston refused. But, after hearing how confident Lasky's people were, he changed his mind. Braddock's next fight was going to be with Art Lasky. He was a young fighter from Minnesota who had won a few fights in the West. He wasn't as fast as Lewis, but he was big and strong.

♦

The Lasky fight started well for Braddock. In the early rounds, his opponent couldn't get past Braddock's gloves. The boxer from Minnesota took a lot of punishment and soon his nose was bloody.

Everything changed in the fifth round. Lasky started hitting Braddock with punch after punch to the body. Fighting with new confidence, he took the next few rounds from the New Jersey man. In the eleventh round, Braddock found himself back on the ropes, as Lasky's fists flew at him.

"Art Lasky is ending the story of Jim Braddock's second chance in boxing," said the radio announcer.

A big punch hit the side of Braddock's head and his mouthguard flew out. The crowd waited for Braddock to drop. Instead, he stood there, eye to eye with Lasky. Then he calmly walked over and picked up his mouthguard.

"I can't believe my eyes," said the announcer. "Braddock just took Lasky's best punch and it had no effect on him!"

Braddock was a different fighter after that. He fought from a distance, throwing jabs at Lasky's bloody face. In the fifteenth round, Braddock's glove hit the other man's nose. Blood showered the ring.

"This is unbelievable!" shouted the radio announcer. "Nothing can stop Braddock now."

As Lasky moved with increasing difficulty, Braddock hit him with a combination of punches that sent him into the ropes at the side of the ring. Those ropes were the only thing that kept Lasky on his feet.

"And the winner is . . . James J. Braddock!"

The shouts of the crowd reached the streets outside. By radio, they reached across the country. They were heard in Branson, Missouri, where Ancil Hoffman ran to another room in the hotel he was staying in. He knocked at the door urgently.

Max Baer, the heavyweight champion of the world, opened the door and looked down angrily at Hoffman.

"Jim Braddock just beat Lasky," said the champion's manager. "He's the number one challenger for your title."

Baer replied with an ugly smile. "The guy's a loser," he said. "Tell Johnston to find me somebody who can fight back." Then he shut the door in Ancil's face.

Chapter 10   Night in the Park

The streets around Madison Square Garden were quiet, but as soon as Jim stepped outside, a crowd of around fifty men closed in around him and Joe. They were very different from the crowd that had waited after the Griffiths fight years ago. These men looked tired and hungry. But when they saw Jim Braddock, hope lit up their faces and they stood taller.

"Just sign your name for a few," said Joe with a smile. "Leave them wanting more."

"No, Joe. Tonight I sign them *all*!"

Jim moved among the crowd, shaking hands and signing his name and talking for over an hour.

Joe did most of the talking on the drive to New Jersey. When they reached the apartment building, Jim opened the door.

"Good night, Joe."

"Haven't you forgotten something?" asked Joe. He reached into his coat for Jim's share of the prize money. He began to explain how he had decided on the amount.

"I trust you, Joe," said Jim. "And Mae trusts you, too."

Joe pushed the money into the fighter's hand and waved goodnight.

When Jim entered the little apartment, he put some of the cash in the jar on the shelf. He put the rest in a white envelope.

Jim didn't sleep much that night and he left the apartment before Mae and the children woke up. The sidewalks were empty as he walked to the center of town. He joined the line inside the relief office and waited patiently.

Finally, he stepped up to the counter and nodded at the woman. He gave her the white envelope.

The woman was confused when she looked at the cash. "So . . . you're giving us the money *back*?"

On the way home, Jim bought twelve roses for Mae. They were

very expensive, but he wanted to apologize for not waking her to tell her about the Lasky fight. He hadn't wanted to celebrate until he had paid back the money to the relief office.

But when he got home, it wasn't the time for celebrating. Mike Wilson's wife, Sara, was sitting on the sofa with her baby girl in her arms. Her eyes were red from crying.

"Mike's gone," said Mae seriously. "It's been three days now."

"About a week after you left the docks, Jim, the foreman stopped picking him for work," cried Sara. "I went to stay with my brother. There wasn't room for Mike, so he's been sleeping in Central Park." Sara looked straight at Jim. "He said he was going to do some work for you. We were going to meet last night, but Mike never came."

Silently, Mae pointed at the jar that contained their money. Jim nodded. "Listen, Sara, you and Mae go and get something for the baby's cough."

But Sara was crying. "Something's wrong. I know it is!"

Jim moved toward the front door. "I'll go and find him."

Hours later, Jim entered Central Park. As the sun sank, he knew that the enormous park wasn't as empty as it looked. Since the Crash of 1929, tens of thousands of New Yorkers were living in cars, or on the streets, or in the subway. A lot of people had started living in Central Park. Some of them built huts or tents from any materials they could find. Others slept wherever they could. They ate any food they could find or catch or steal.

Jim had heard that there had been a lot of sheep in Central Park. Most had been moved away. Now, as he searched for Mike, Jim saw park workers guiding the last sheep into enormous wagons. Jim watched until a policeman on a horse waved at him to move away.

The shadows became longer as night came, and soon trash can fires were the only lights in the park. Jim went deeper into the park, past huts and tents. The sound of wet coughs filled the air.

"Mike! Mike Wilson?" he called.

Suddenly, two running policemen shouted at him to get out of the way. He looked to see where they were going and saw a crowd of people around several policemen on horses. Jim heard angry shouts and saw flames. He ran to the crowd and had to push his way through a wall of people to reach the center.

A group of men had fought the police here, turning one of the sheep wagons over and burning huts. The police were in control again and were guiding the men away like sheep.

There were two policemen on horses near Jim. "We were just trying to move the sheep," one of them told the other. "But one of these guys started shouting at us. He was angry, very political. Then they attacked us."

Jim closed his eyes and remembered all Mike's angry talk. He knew this must be Mike. He began looking for his friend among all the fallen men on the grass. He got closer to the wagon that lay on its side.

"A guy tried to free the sheep," a policeman was saying. "The horses were scared and the wagon turned over."

There was someone with his legs under the enormous wheels of the wagon. A group of men lifted the wagon up, and that's when Jim realized that there was a second man under the wagon, lying in a pool of blood. It was Mike.

Jim's friend wasn't dead yet. Jim moved the hair from Mike's eyes.

"Did you win?" Mike asked. His voice was soft and filled with pain.

Jim nodded. "You're going to be OK, Mike," he said.

Mike managed a weak nod. "I know it . . ."

But, in the cold and dark of New York's Central Park, as the smoke from the burning huts blew over them and took away the last of the light, both men knew that this wasn't true.

♦

Few people came to Mike's funeral. It was a work day and most people couldn't afford to lose a day's money. Only Jim and Mae Braddock and their three children stood with Sara Wilson and her baby daughter as Mike's body was put into the ground.

Jim spoke of Mike's love for his family, his wife. He didn't say what he felt—that Mike's death was a waste, a stupid, unnecessary waste. Jim understood why people got angry, but Mike's anger hadn't helped his wife or his daughter. Jim wished he had known how bad things had become for his friend. He couldn't forget how kind Mike had been to him when he started working at the docks.

Mae's attention was on Sara, whose eyes were far away. She seemed to be staring into the long future that waited for her without her husband.

As she looked at Sara, part of Mae wondered if she was looking into a mirror of her own future. Maybe not today or tomorrow— but one day she might lose Jim.

Chapter 11   Face to Face with the Champion

Madison Square Garden, March 24, 1935

Jim Braddock and Joe Gould smiled for the cameras. Then it was time for the reporters' questions.

"Jim, do you have anything to say to our readers?"

"Not everybody gets a second chance," answered Jim. He looked at Mae, who sat at the front in a new yellow dress, smiling nervously. "I have a lot to be grateful for."

A second reporter stood. "Can you tell our readers why you gave your relief money back?"

Jim nodded. "This great country of ours helps a man when he's in trouble. I've had some good luck, so I thought I'd return the money."

Another reporter stood. "Max Baer says that he's worried he's going to kill you in the ring. What do you say?"

Mae looked down at her hands. Jim looked the reporter in the eye. "Max Baer is the champion," he said. "I'm looking forward to the fight."

The next question was from a familiar face. Sporty Lewis stood and turned toward Mae. "Mrs. Braddock, how do you feel about the fact that Max Baer has killed two men in the ring?" Mae could find no words. "Mrs. Braddock, are you scared for your husband's life?" continued Lewis.

A camera appeared in front of Mae's face. Jim jumped to his feet. "She's scared for Max Baer!" he shouted.

Joe Gould lifted his arms like a referee. "OK, OK, one more question . . ."

While Jim answered the last question, his eyes searched for Mae. She refused to look up, not wanting him to see the doubts and fear in her eyes.

♦

When Jim Braddock and Joe Gould entered Madison Square Garden's boxing club, Jimmy Johnston was waiting for them. The rich, powerful businessman waved a newspaper at the fighter and his manager.

"It says here that this fight is as good as murder," Johnston said, stepping close up to Braddock. "This is my business, and I'm going to protect myself. You *will* know exactly what Baer can do before you get in that ring."

A door opened and a small man in a suit entered the room. This was Johnston's lawyer, and he was followed by a secretary.

Johnston went to a machine and began to show a film. It showed two boxers getting ready to fight. One was Max Baer. Johnston said the other man's name. "That's Frankie Campbell . . . A good fighter who knows how to take a punch."

The fight began. Johnston turned to Braddock. "Is Campbell's style familiar, Jim? It's like looking in a mirror, isn't it?"

"He doesn't need to see this," complained Joe.

"He'll see it or there'll be no fight!" Johnston warned.

On the film, Campbell stepped forward with a good left jab, almost as good as Jim's. Baer blocked it easily, then hit back with his right. The punch was too fast to see, and it had a strange, terrible power. Campbell just stood there in confusion, with his gloves down by his side. The second punch hit the side of his head. And then Campbell was down, his legs wide, his eyes open but seeing nothing.

"It was the second punch that killed him," said Johnston.

"You've warned us," said Joe. "Now stop the film."

"No," said Jim, surprising both Joe and Johnston. "Show it again."

When the lights were back on, Johnston stared at Jim. "Remember Ernie Schaff? He was a good fighter. Ernie took one of Baer's punches on the chin. He was dead and didn't know it. In his next fight, the first jab killed him." He sat back in his chair. "Do you want to think about this fight?"

Jim hit his hands on the desk angrily. "Do you think you're telling me something I don't know?" he shouted. "How many guys died because they didn't have enough food? Or because they had to work long hours and dangerous jobs to feed their families? I've thought about it as much as I'm going to."

"OK, then." Johnston looked away. "Why don't you both eat here tonight with your wives?"

The fight organizer smiled, but there was something about the look in his eyes that Jim didn't trust.

Later that day, the two men returned to the club's restaurant with their wives. The four ate, talked, and laughed, as a piano played quietly in the corner.

After the meal, Joe pulled a newspaper out of his pocket. He turned to the sports pages and began to read. "Jim Braddock is back from the dead to give hope to every American."

Jim was surprised. "Who wrote that?"

"Sporty Lewis. The newspaper is calling you the Cinderella Man."

"Cinderella Man?" Jim didn't look happy. *Cinderella* was a children's story. Wasn't Cinderella the girl who had to stay at home and clean while her sisters went to a wonderful party at the palace?

"I like it," said Mae, squeezing his hand.

Suddenly, an enormous man with two young women on his arms walked in through the front door. Conversations died around the room. The man had thick black hair and the brightest blue eyes. He was wearing an expensive white jacket, but he looked dangerous. As usual, all eyes in the room turned to him. This was Max Baer.

Jim turned to his manager. "Do you think Johnston planned this?" he asked angrily.

Joe nodded. "Sure. More pictures for the papers."

Physically, Baer was the perfect boxer. He had a narrow waist, wide shoulders, strong legs, and long arms. He was young, too—at twenty-six, three years younger than Jim. And he had the strongest punch Joe Gould had ever seen—probably the strongest punch in the history of boxing.

Joe knew that there were ways to beat the champion. His right-hand punch was so powerful that he hadn't really worked on improving his left hand. But Joe couldn't forget the sight of Baer destroying Primo Carnera. The big Italian had been knocked down eleven times in that fight.

Joe's attention moved away from Baer when a waiter arrived with a bottle of wine and four glasses.

"From the gentleman at the bar . . . Mr. Baer said I should wish you good luck."

Jim looked at Mae. The blood had run from her face, leaving her pale with worry. He stood. "Get the coats, Joe." Then he began walking toward the bar.

Baer gave a big smile when he saw Jim coming. "Look, it's the Cinderella Man!" he shouted.

Jim stood toe to toe with the champion. "You keep saying in the newspapers that you're going to kill me in the ring. I have three little kids. You're upsetting my family."

Baer moved closer. His voice was quiet as he said, "Listen to me, Braddock. I'm asking you not to take this fight. People admire you. You seem like a nice guy, and I don't want to hurt you. It's no joke. They're calling you the Cinderella Man. Well, people die in children's stories all the time."

Suddenly, a small crowd of reporters and photographers ran into the club. Baer turned to face the cameras and smiled. His voice was loud again as he started performing for the cameras. "If you're smart, you'll fall over in the first round," he told Jim.

Jim's eyes met Baer's. "I think I'll try for a few rounds," he said.

Baer noticed Mae, standing behind Jim now. "You should talk to him," he said. "You're much too pretty to lose your husband." Jim squeezed his fist into a ball, ready to attack, but Baer continued to look at Mae. "Maybe I can take care of you after he's gone."

This time Joe Gould jumped, waving his fists at the champion. Jim pulled him back.

Mae stepped up to the bar. Baer's bright blue eyes followed her as she picked up his drink, then threw it in his face.

Baer just laughed as he dried his face. "Did you get that, boys?" he said to the reporters. "Braddock has his wife fighting for him."

Jim stepped up to Max Baer. The two boxers were nose to nose. Then Jim turned, took his wife's hand, and led her away. As they left, the sound of Baer laughing followed them into the street.

53

Chapter 12   The Big Day

"Keep your head down and give me a combination—left, right, left."

Jim was teaching Jay and Howard how to box. Jay threw out a right fist and lifted his chin. Jim reached forward and gently hit his son's chin. "Don't take your eyes off your opponent," he said.

"That's enough, now," said Mae from the kitchen sink.

Jim looked at his boys proudly. "There's more than one fighter in the Braddock family."

As the two boys continued to box, they knocked over a chair.

Mae turned. "I said that's enough!" she cried. "No boxing in the house!" She pointed at her two sons. "You are going to stay in school. Then college. You are going to have professions. You are not going to have your heads broken in the boxing ring. Is that clear?"

The boys froze. Before they could reply, Mae ran out of the apartment. As she stood outside, she could still hear Sporty Lewis's words in her head: *Max Baer has killed two men in the ring.*

She didn't turn when she heard Jim's steps. "When you boxed before, sometimes I hoped that you would get hurt. Just enough so you couldn't fight again . . . I always knew a day would come when a fight could kill you. And now it's here." She looked her husband in the eye. "Why? Why fight him?"

"This is what I know how to do," said Jim simply.

Mae waited for Jim to take her in his arms, to say that he had changed his mind, but he didn't. Part of him wished that he could, but it was impossible. She didn't understand how it felt for men like Jim or Mike Wilson—strong, hardworking men who were told that they were useless. There were thousands of people like this now, and they found hope in the fighter they called the Cinderella Man. Jim had to fight, for them.

Mae's fear turned to anger. "I supported you until now," she said. "But not for this, Jim. I just can't . . ." Her voice went cold. "You find a way out of this fight. Break your hand again, if you have to. But if you leave this apartment to fight Max Baer, I won't support you."

◆

As the day of the fight grew closer, Max Baer helped reporters fill their sports pages. His latest demand was that there must be an ambulance outside Madison Square Garden, ready to rush Jim to a local hospital after Baer hit him.

Jim just continued training. Joe Jeannette chose good partners for him to work with in the ring. Each one helped Jim improve one skill—one partner helped him work on his hand speed; another partner allowed him to practice dodging big punches; another helped him move around the ring quickly.

Jim, Joe, and Jeannette also watched film of Baer's fights for hours every day. "Watch him," said Jeannette, pointing. "His punches are strong, but you can see them coming."

With just a few weeks to go, Braddock's training became even harder. Joe and Jeannette started changing his boxing partners more and more often, so Jim fought a fresh fighter every round. One of the newspaper sports pages included something that Joe had said: "Braddock is going to be really prepared for this fight, if he lives through training!"

Joe laughed when he read that, until his wife reminded him that Mae Braddock would read it, too.

◆

Finally, the big day arrived. When Joe Gould arrived at the gym that morning, Jim was sitting alone, with a jacket tight around his chest.

"What's wrong with him?" the manager asked Joe Jeannette.

Jeannette shook his head. "He's fitter than ever, but he's old. His ribs aren't strong since the Lasky fight."

Gould already knew about the problem with Jim's ribs, but he thought there was something else wrong. Gould knew that Jim's wife wasn't happy about his profession, and about this fight especially. But whatever the problem was, there was no time to solve it now. The fight was just hours away.

"The reporters will be here soon," he told Jim. "Take off that jacket or Baer will see that you have a rib problem."

Jim climbed into the training ring as a crowd of sports writers rushed into the room. He worked hard, but he still wanted to train more after the last reporter had gone.

Joe Jeannette refused. "Go home and get some rest. You'll be working hard enough in the ring tonight."

So Jim went home. He returned to a house that was empty except for Mae. She stood silently, looking at the newspaper:

WORLD CHAMPION FIGHT TONIGHT
MANY WORRY FOR BRADDOCK'S LIFE

Without a word, she turned and walked away.

As the morning became afternoon, Jim lay in bed, unable to sleep. A taxi came for him at four o'clock.

Mae followed Jim outside, where a small crowd of neighbors was waiting: "Come home with that title!" "Knock him out!"

Jim kissed his three children. Then his eyes met Mae's. "I can't win if you don't support me," he said.

"Then don't go, Jimmy."

Time seemed to stretch, with each of them waiting for the other to say something. Then Mae turned and pulled the children close to her. Jim watched as she pushed her way back through the crowd. Then he climbed into the waiting taxi.

The taxi drove past the tall buildings of Manhattan, then crossed the East River. Jim was silent, running the films of Baer's fights through his head, remembering Jeannette's advice—anything to help him forget the look on Mae's face as he left.

They reached the Madison Square Garden Bowl and Jim looked out at the waiting crowd. He could see that these people had known hard times. But there was something else, too, a bright look in their eyes—hope.

Jim saw his own face in the glass of the car window. He had beaten Tuffy Griffiths so confidently, but that man was gone forever. He had passed his hat hopelessly around the boxing club, but that man, was gone, too. No, he was looking now at the face of every man who had ever been beaten down by hard times but refused to stop fighting.

That's when Jim knew. No matter what happened tonight, he wouldn't give up. He would die trying.

♦

It was a hot day and getting hotter. Jim sat in his dressing room waiting to go out and be weighed.

"Come on, champion," said Joe Gould when there was a knock on the door.

"Wait a minute," said Jim. "The last time I looked, I was the challenger, not the champion."

"I know what I said," replied Joe.

On his way to the weighing room, Max Baer had seen an old trainer who had worked with him years before. There were angry words and Baer hit out at the man. Cameras recorded the attack.

When there was peace in the room again, officials and reporters watched the two boxers being weighed. It was very hot in the crowded room.

Max Baer went first, stepping up with his fists above his head and an ugly smile on his face.

"Ninety-five and a half kilograms," the judge announced.

Then it was Jim's turn. "Eighty-six and a half kilograms."

Max Baer was waiting for him when he stepped down. "How does the story go?" said Baer, loud enough for all the reporters to hear. "The clock strikes midnight, and then Cinderella loses her skirt!"

People laughed and more photos were taken, but Jim didn't care. He would have the chance to reply later, in the ring. He went back to his dressing room to get ready for the fight.

Max Baer returned to his dressing room. His trainer was waiting with something for the champion to watch—a film of Braddock's fight against Art Lasky.

"Look, right there!" said the trainer, as Lasky hit Braddock in the ribs, clearly hurting him. "Braddock's ribs are weak. If you can hit them with a few good jabs, you'll really hurt him."

"I don't need to," answered Baer. "I can knock this loser down any time. I just need to give the crowd a good show before I kill him."

Baer's manager, Ancil Hoffman, came into the room.

"Did you get it?" asked the champion.

Hoffman nodded. "The ambulance is waiting outside. There's a doctor there, too."

Max looked in the mirror. "That's all I can do for him. Now Braddock's on his own."

◆

Mae spent the rest of the day at her sister's house. As the children played, she and Alice sat and talked, but they didn't discuss the real reason for Mae's visit.

As the afternoon shadows grew longer, Mae became quieter. At five o'clock, she stood. "No radio, Alice," she said. "I'll be back soon."

Mae walked through the empty streets of Newark until she came to the family's church. Father Rorick stood at the door. There were crowds inside.

"Father?" Mae asked, confused by the crowd. "I came to say a few words in church for Jim."

"All these people are doing the same," said the priest. "They think Jim's fighting for them."

Mae looked at the crowd again. All of these people were beaten down by hard times. They admired her husband. If he could fight and win, maybe *they* could . . .

"Yes, I understand now," said Mae. She turned and hurried down the street. She could hear radios through open windows and doors. Everybody was getting ready to listen to the fight— at the docks, in homes and bars, in Sam the butcher's. Beyond Newark, too—across the country—people wanted the Cinderella Man to win. They wanted him to become the prince, the king, the *champion*.

◆

Joe Gould was taping Jim's hands in the dressing room. They could hear the sound of the crowd beyond. Suddenly, there was a knock on the door and a small, familiar shape stood there—it was Mae.

"Excuse me for a minute," said Joe. He left, closing the door behind him.

Finally, Mae spoke. "You can't win if I don't support you."

"I keep telling you that," said Jim.

Mae handed him a brown paper bag. "I thought it was going to rain, so I used the money in the rainy-day jar." Jim opened the bag and stared at the new pair of boxing shoes inside.

"Maybe I understand." Mae's eyes shone. The two kissed and, smiling through her tears, Mae said, "I always support you, Jimmy. Just you remember who you are! You're everybody's hope and your kids' hero and you're the champion of my heart, James J. Braddock!"

It was almost fight time. "See you at home, okay?" Mae whispered, as she moved to the door. "Please, Jimmy . . ."

Jim nodded. "See you at home."

Chapter 13   The Hopes of the Crowd

Madison Square Garden Bowl, Long Island City,
New York, June 13, 1935

As Jim Braddock stepped out into the bright lights, the crowd became silent. The ring seemed so far away. Between him and it were thousands of people—Jim's people. He knew the looks on their faces—people who saw no chance of a future. Some had spent their last dollar to be here, but tonight they all held their heads high. Their eyes followed him with the wild hope that the story of the Cinderella Man would have a happy ending.

It was the strangest walk to the ring Jim had ever made. As he passed, people got to their feet. They smiled and nodded and waved at their hero, but they were still silent. Finally, someone called his name and the shout broke the silence for everybody. The whole crowd—thirty-five thousand people—began to shout, and the noise went up to the star-filled sky.

♦

Mae's sister Alice was looking for Jay, Howard, and Rosy, to call them to supper. There was no sign of the children. Were they hiding? She was going to look outside, when she heard a sound from the closet under the stairs.

All three children were sitting around a radio. They looked up at their aunt, and Alice knew that she couldn't stop them. Without saying a word, she sat down next to the children and listened to the announcer on the radio.

"I don't know if you can hear me," the announcer was shouting. "I can't hear myself! The crowd is on its feet and the noise is deafening."

Back in the Madison Square Garden Bowl, the crowd was silent again when they realized that Max Baer was walking to the ring. The champion felt the crowd's fear. He enjoyed it. When he had climbed into the ring, Baer ran around and accepted the crowd's boos with a confident smile on his face.

The referee called the boxers and their corner men to him. "I want a clean fight," he said. "When I say break, step back immediately. And remember"—he looked at Jim—"protect yourself at all times."

As the fighters touched gloves, Baer's corner man held a gold watch in front of Braddock's face. "One minute to midnight, Cinderella!" he laughed.

The fighters returned to their corners. Baer's manager, Ancil Hoffman, whispered final words of advice to the champion, but Baer wasn't interested. Jim closed his eyes. Finally, the sound of the bell broke the silence and the fight began.

♦

Round 1 Braddock came out fast and hard, hoping to surprise the champion. Showing no fear, he hit Baer with a right hand, and then followed it with a left to the body. The champion tried to punch back, but Braddock danced away.

On Braddock's next attack, Baer was ready. His left fist hit Braddock's ribs hard. Braddock's answer was a combination of punches—a long right to the face, another right, a left, and a final right to the chin. The champion knew now that Braddock had a good punch, but he refused to show any pain.

"Calm down, old man," Baer laughed as the fighters held on to each other. "I'll let the fight go a few rounds."

As the bell rang, Baer knew that he had lost the round on points, but he didn't care. He was confident that he could end this fight at any time with one punch.

In the corner, Gould met Braddock with a big smile. "Did you see the look on Baer's face when you hit him?"

Jim took out his mouthguard. "Yes, he was *laughing*."

"So use your left hand to knock that smile off his face!"

In the opposite corner Ancil Hoffman was shouting, but Baer waved him away. "I'll kill him when I'm ready."

"Your left, Jimmy," Joe said again. "Remember your left."

Round 2 Braddock came out with his fists moving at the start of the second round, too.

"Nobody expected this fight to go one round," the radio announcer was saying. "But it's only reached round two because Baer is playing with Braddock. He's thrown almost no punches and he's laughing at the challenger."

But soon Baer started throwing more punches, aiming at Braddock's weak ribs. The strength of Baer's punches knocked the breath out of him.

"The champion has really hurt the challenger," said the announcer. The crowd began to boo.

"That's the right place, isn't it, old man?" said Baer.

The referee separated the fighters at the sound of the bell. One of Braddock's corner men worked on the fighter's cuts, while the other gave the boxer water. Jim coughed it back up. He needed air, not water.

Joe examined Jim's ribs. "They're not broken," he said. "Not yet."

Across the ring, Baer was playing and acting for the cameras. As he watched this, Jim realized that he himself didn't care about pleasing the crowd now. He wasn't even fighting Baer. He was fighting to beat the thing that had beaten him. He was fighting for his family's future.

Round 3 For the third time, Braddock came out fast. He threw his punches at Baer's head, but the champion's punches were aimed at his opponent's body. Baer continued to hit Braddock's ribs hard with both hands. He hit Braddock with a low punch, and the referee warned the champion to keep his fists up.

Before the fight started again, Gould saw that Braddock's gloves were down by his side, but there was no time to shout a warning.

Baer had seen it, too. He hit the side of Braddock's head with a big left-hand punch. Jim's legs bent. He was clearly in terrible pain—was he going to fall? Gould froze in fear. He thought about giving in, ending the fight.

"Give him a chance, Joe," said the corner man.

A few seconds later, Jim stood straighter and reached for the ropes.

Baer couldn't believe it. He attacked again, but this time Braddock hit back with a long right, then a left jab that made Baer's head look like a punching bag.

"That's it!" shouted Gould, jumping up and down.

Round 4 From the start of the next round, both men stood toe to toe, throwing jabs. Braddock's feet were quicker and his punches more effective, so Baer started aiming for the body again. After a few good punches to the ribs, he was sure that every breath caused Braddock terrible pain.

The two men held each other again and the referee called for them to break. But Baer continued to hold Braddock.

"Dirty fighting!" shouted Gould angrily from the corner.

"I warned you," the referee told Baer. "When I say 'Break!' you break!"

The crowd booed as Baer finally stepped back. He shook the sweat from his thick black hair and held up his hands to apologize. Out of the corner of his eye, he could see that Braddock wasn't protecting himself.

Without warning, Baer turned and delivered an enormous punch to Braddock's ribs. To everybody's surprise—especially Baer's —Braddock replied with a combination of left-right punches before stepping back.

Round 5 Baer's manager, Ancil Hoffman, couldn't understand it. The challenger's ribs were in bad condition, but Braddock was still controlling the fight, jabbing Baer again and again and tiring him. The timing of the champion's punches wasn't right, and Hoffman knew that he was waiting for the chance to deliver his big knockout punch instead of tiring his opponent. But Baer wasn't able to hit Braddock, who dodged and danced away skillfully.

The champion was getting angry now. He hit Braddock with an illegal backhand punch as the referee separated the two fighters. The referee warned Baer, but the two men continued fighting before holding on to each other again.

"Step back!" shouted the referee, but the two men didn't let go.

Braddock hit the champion's chin with his head. The champion shouted in anger. He lifted Braddock and threw him into the ropes, paying no attention to the boos of the crowd.

When the round was over, Hoffman shouted angrily at Baer, "What are you doing?"

"Relax," the champion told him.

"I'll relax," replied Ancil, "when we walk out of here with the title."

Round 6 Baer hit Braddock with three good punches in the first seconds of the round. Blood poured from the challenger's nose and mouth.

But then, suddenly, it seemed to Baer that a train had hit him. It was Braddock's right hand, and it hit the champion on the chin with enormous power. Baer stepped back, fighting for air. But Braddock gave him no space, throwing punch after punch with his left hand. One of them hit the champion just above the eye. Baer fought back, but his aim wasn't as good as the challenger's. His right eye began to close.

For the first time in this fight, Baer felt relief when the bell rang. He promised himself that he would end the fight in the next round, even if he had to kill the Cinderella Man to do it.

Round 7 As soon as the round began, it was clear that Baer had a new attitude. Joe Gould could see it. The crowd could also feel the change. Baer wanted to finish this fight *now*.

But Braddock wasn't afraid. He met the champion in the middle of the ring and the two fighters continued the fight. Baer hit Braddock with several punches to the body. The last of these hit below the belt.

"Keep your punches up, Max," said Braddock.

Baer smiled and delivered a combination of punches to his opponent's body and head. "Is that *up* enough?"

Braddock forced himself to smile through the pain. "That's fine, Max."

As the bell rang, Baer continued throwing punches. Braddock hit back as hard as he could, but Max Baer just laughed.

"I can't believe this!" said the radio announcer. "Everybody expected the champion to win easily. But now, after the seventh round, neither fighter is ahead. Either of them could win."

Chapter 14   The Luckiest Man

"Alice?" The house seemed empty. Mae looked at the uneaten meal on her sister's kitchen table. Then she heard noises from the closet in the hall. They were all there—Mae's three children and her sister—listening to the fight on the radio.

"The crowd was expecting big things from champion Max Baer in the eighth round," the radio announcer was saying. "But Jim Braddock refused to be beaten."

Rosy looked up and saw her mother. "It's the police," she said to the others.

"By the ninth round, it was a fact that Braddock had fought better than anybody expected," continued the announcer. "But some people were saying that Baer allowed this to happen. In the tenth round, the champion was in complete control of the fight."

Mae reached to turn off the radio. Jay's eyes met hers. "Please, Mom."

She looked into their hopeful faces and knew that she couldn't say no. But she refused to listen herself. Without a word, she turned and walked away, as the eleventh round began.

Round 11 Baer was mad as he rushed out. He chased Braddock around the ring, throwing punches at the challenger . . . and then it came—Baer's big punch, the one that had killed two men.

When it hit him, Braddock's mind was in a fog. He felt heavy and light at the same time, and his legs could only just support him. He felt the ropes on his back.

Suddenly, a memory of his family came into Jim's head—his wife and children. The reason why he was here. He let the ropes support him for a few seconds, and then he pushed forward, back on his feet.

Baer just stared at Braddock, unable to believe that the challenger had taken the punch and not been knocked out. Jim looked back into Baer's broken face and smiled.

For the rest of the round, Baer tried to finish his opponent, but his wild punches missed. Braddock hit back with a jab, a cross, another jab. With each punch, he felt his strength returning. There was blood on Baer's face now.

At the end of the round, Braddock's corner men worked urgently on the cut under the fighter's eye. Joe Gould seemed close to tears. "Jimmy," said his manager. "Win, or lose . . ."

"Thanks, Joe, for all of it." Jim lifted a bloody glove. "Now stop talking."

Round 12 Baer started the twelfth round still trying to finish the fight with one big punch. But the challenger was faster and dodged the punches.

"He's slow!" shouted Gould from the corner.

The crowd was shouting in both happiness and fear.

"You're right, it *is* a funeral," shouted the young reporter next to Sporty Lewis. "Max Baer's funeral."

But Lewis didn't hear. He was on his feet, shouting like everybody else. The crowd's shout was like a wave of noise.

"Braddock! Braddock! Braddock!"

It was too much for Max Baer. He ran at Braddock, moving his fists fast and hard. The punches hit the challenger, the last one below the belt. Braddock bent over in pain as the round ended.

Joe Gould jumped over the ropes, shouting angrily at Baer. The referee and the fight's doctor had to lift the little manager back out of the ring.

Baer just stood in the center of the ring.

"That low punch lost you the round," the referee told him.

Baer waved him away and moved back to his corner. Ancil Hoffman was waiting for him. "You're losing! Are you listening to me? Do you want to lose the title to this nobody?"

♦

At her sister's house in New Jersey, Mae had stopped pretending to herself that she was reading the newspaper—that she wasn't listening to the radio.

She went back to the hall, where the others still sat listening. Mae hid around the corner so her children couldn't see her. She stood in the dark and listened to the thirteenth and fourteenth rounds with growing fear.

At last, when there was just one more round in the fight, she stepped out of the shadows. Rosy moved to the side. "Sit here, Mommy." Mae joined her children. Pale with worry, she listened to the announcer.

"It's the fifteenth and final round. The crowd is shouting at Braddock to stay away because Baer is looking for the knockout . . . but Braddock is not staying away, and Baer is delivering the biggest punches of his life."

Mae saw the fear now in her children's eyes. Would their father come home tonight?

"But Braddock is not only standing . . . he's coming forward!"

Round 15 In the ring, Max Baer and Jim Braddock were beaten, bloody and tired. They fought for air as they circled each other, looking for a chance to get past their opponent's defenses. Baer's fists flew and all of his punches were strong enough to knock a man out, but they were wild and anxious. Braddock remained on his feet. He kept coming forward, bringing the fight to Baer.

The final seconds of the fight seemed to stretch forever. For the boxers, the crowd seemed to disappear; the referee, the judges, and the managers were gone, too. For each man there was only the other fighter.

Braddock danced to the side and threw a jab. Baer saw his chance. He threw his famous right punch and hit Braddock right in the head. It knocked the challenger to the side, and now Baer could hit him with the second punch. Silence fell over the crowd. Was this the end?

No. Braddock turned and just managed to dodge the next punch. He hit back, and the two men were still throwing punches when the final bell rang. The fight had ended!

Everybody waited to hear the fight officials announce a winner. It was clear which fighter the crowd wanted.

"Braddock! Braddock! Braddock!"

Minutes later, Braddock was still resting on the ropes while the fight doctor examined him and Joe Gould took his boxing gloves off.

"I don't like it," said Joe. "The judges are taking too long."

A shadow fell across their corner. It was Max Baer, who looked Jim Braddock in the eye. "You beat me. It doesn't matter what they say."

Jim tried to find the right words, but Baer was gone before he had a chance to say them.

At last, the judges handed a small, white card to the fight announcer. He climbed over the ropes and moved to the microphone in the middle of the ring.

"Ladies and gentlemen, the winner . . . and new heavyweight champion of the world . . ."

The rest of his words were lost in an explosion of noise.

The same noise filled the streets of Newark. People poured from their houses into the streets to celebrate. They poured out of Father Rorick's church to join everybody else in an unplanned street party. People laughed and cried with happiness. Faces that looked old with worry became suddenly young again.

At her sister's house, Mae's cry cut the night. As the family celebrated, little Rosy smiled proudly at her mother. "It's the steak," she said.

Back at the Madison Square Garden Bowl, the crowd pushed forward for a better look at the Cinderella Man. Everybody wanted to shake his hand, to touch him, to take home a little of his magic for themselves.

James J. Braddock stood in the center of the ring with his arms lifted over his head. Tears poured from his eyes. He listened to the crowd's shouts, but his heart was in another place. It was in a little New Jersey apartment, where his wife and three children would soon be waiting for him to come home. In the end, they were the reason why he was not only the heavyweight champion of the world, but also the luckiest man in it.

♦

And so James J. Braddock, at the age of 29, became heavyweight champion of the world on June 13, 1935. None of the judges disagreed with the decision. For the public and the press, his win was one of the biggest surprises in the history of the sport. Most agreed that Baer had been beaten by a better boxer on the night.

For two years, Braddock didn't box again. Finally, a fight was arranged with Joe Louis, the "Brown Bomber" from Detroit. On June 22, 1937, the two fighters met in Chicago.

By this time, Braddock was not as strong or healthy as he had been. His left arm was very weak, but he still managed to knock Louis down in the first round. By the fourth round, Joe Louis was controlling the fight. According to Braddock, "After a couple of rounds, I knew I was in there with a great fighter." The end came when Louis knocked Braddock out in the eighth round. "When he hit me with that right, I just lay there." Joe Louis later became one of the greatest heavyweight title holders in the history of boxing.

James J. Braddock fought one more fight after that, in 1938, against a young boxer from Wales, Tommy Farr. Farr had lasted all fifteen rounds against Louis, and most people expected him to beat Braddock. Again, Braddock surprised everybody by winning the fight. Then he decided to leave the sport as a winner. "I have won my last fight," he announced to the press.

After he stopped boxing, Jim Braddock remained friends with Joe Gould. And Braddock had a lot to thank his manager for. When Gould had allowed Joe Louis to challenge Braddock for the title in 1937, he had demanded money from all Joe Louis's heavyweight title fights for the next ten years if Louis won. Jim and Mae Braddock were never poor again. The couple lived in the same New Jersey house that they bought after Jim won the heavyweight title. Jim spent the rest of his life surrounded by friends and neighbors who admired and loved him.

Looking back, Jim Braddock said that, when Baer hit him with his best punch and Jim didn't fall, he was "the happiest guy in the world." The story of the Cinderella Man did have a happy ending.

ACTIVITIES

Chapter 1

Before you read

1 Do you like to watch boxing? Why (not)? Discuss the sport with another student. Who is or was your country's greatest boxer?

2 Look at the Word List at the back of the book. Check the meaning of unfamiliar words; then discuss these questions with another student. Use the Internet or library books to help you if you don't know much about boxing.

   a Who is or was the greatest heavyweight champion in the history of boxing? Why?

   b In your opinion, how many rounds should there be in an amateur boxing fight? How many should there be in a professional fight? Why?

   c If a boxer is being hit often and is not throwing any punches back, should the referee always stop the fight? Why (not)?

   d What would you like to be the world champion of? Why?

   e When is the last time you heard people booing? Why were they booing?

   f In your opinion, which of these jobs is the hardest? Why?
      butcher   priest   worker at the docks   boxer

3 Read the Introduction to the book and answer these questions.

   a What caused hard times in the U.S. in the 1930s?

   b How was Jim Braddock like millions of other unlucky Americans?

   c Why did actor Russell Crowe want to play Braddock?

   d How did Crowe train for the film?

While you read

4 Are these sentences correct? Write *yes* or *no*.

   a Jim Braddock is expected to beat Tuffy Griffiths.   .....

   b Braddock wins the fight by a knockout.   .....

   c Joe Gould decides which boxers fight at Madison
      Square Garden.   .....

   d Braddock was born in New Jersey.   .....

71

e	Braddock still lives in New Jersey.	.....
f	Jim likes to go to clubs after a fight.	.....
g	Joe Gould likes to see Mae Braddock.	.....
h	Mae refused to marry Jim until he had enough money.	.....
i	Jim and Mae have three children.	.....
j	Mae goes to all of Jim's fights.	.....

After you read

5 Discuss how these people feel about each other. Give reasons for your answers.

a Jim and Joe   **c** Jim and Mae

b Joe and Jimmy Johnston   **d** Joe and Mae

6 Describe Mae's attitude to Jim's job. How would you feel in her situation?

Chapters 2–3

Before you read

7 Life changed for many Americans on October 29, 1929. What do you think happened on that day? What happened afterward?

8 You are going to read about the Braddock family's money problems. How do you think these will affect Jim? How will they affect Mae?

9 Jim's next fight is described as "an embarrassment." Why, do you think?

While you read

10 Write the name of the character.

a	Who is afraid about Jim's next fight?	....
b	Who pulls out a gun at the docks?	....
c	Who steals food?	....
d	Who promises that the Braddocks will never send their children away?	....
e	Who says he will buy Jim an ice cream?	....
f	Whose hand is broken?	....
g	Who takes away Jim's license?	....
h	Who tells Jim, "It's finished"?	....

After you read

11 How has life changed for Jim and his family since 1928? Make a list and compare it with the lists of other students.

12 Why are these important to the story?
Jim and Mae's wedding picture   a jar   a piece of meat

13 Work in pairs and have these conversations.
   Student A: You are Jim Braddock. Pick one of these times in the story and tell your friend what your thoughts are.
   a   waiting for work at the docks
   b   before the Feldman fight
   c   after you lost your license
   Student B: You are Jim's friend. Ask questions.

Chapters 4–5

Before you read

14 Look at the titles of these chapters and discuss the questions.
   a   What will Jim's new life be like? How do you think he will earn money for his family with a broken right hand?
   b   What promise will be broken? Who will break it?

15 In Chapter 5, Jimmy goes back to Madison Square Garden, but not as a boxer. Why do you think he goes there? Think of some possible reasons.

While you read

16 Number these events in the correct order, from 1 to 10.
   a   Jim sells his boxing shoes at the gym.   . . . . .
   b   Joe Gould gives Jim money.   . . . . .
   c   Mae takes the children to her relatives.   . . . . .
   d   Jim is chosen to work at the docks.   . . . . .
   e   The electricity is turned back on.   . . . . .
   f   The Braddocks' electricity is cut off.   . . . . .
   g   Jim goes to the relief office.   . . . . .
   h   Jim covers his cast with black shoe polish.   . . . . .
   i   Jim and Mike help a young couple.   . . . . .
   j   Jim meets Mike Wilson.   . . . . .

After you read

17 Why:

    a does Mike Wilson help Jim at the docks?

    b doesn't Joe Gould speak to Jim when he sees him at the gym?

    c does Mae take the children to her relatives?

    d does Jim become angry that the children are gone?

18 You are Jim Braddock. Pick one of these times in the story and tell the class your thoughts.

    a working at the docks

    b seeing Joe Jeannette at the gym

    c in the line at the relief office

    d when the electricity is turned back on

Chapters 6–7

Before you read

19 Discuss these questions with another student.

    a In Chapter 6, Joe Gould offers Jim something. What will this be?

    b In Chapter 7, Joe Gould says, "Where have you been, Jimmy Braddock?" Why do you think he says this?

While you read

20 Read the questions and circle YES or NO.

a	Is it Howard's birthday?	YES	NO
b	Had Jim hit the priest?	YES	NO
c	Does Jim hit Mike Wilson?	YES	NO
d	Is Mae happy about the children boxing?	YES	NO
e	Is Mae happy about the Griffin fight?	YES	NO
f	Does Jim train hard for the Griffin fight?	YES	NO
g	Does Jim fight Corn Griffin on an empty stomach?	YES	NO
h	Does Sporty Lewis think that Jim will win?	YES	NO
i	Does Jim beat Griffin by a knockout?	YES	NO
j	Does Max Baer beat Primo Carnera?	YES	NO

After you read

21 Answer these questions.

    a Why is there a party at the church?

    b Why does Joe come to see Jim at his apartment?

    c Why do the Braddock children go back to the butcher shop?

    d Why does Joe Gould look for a spoon?

    e Why does Sporty Lewis get a surprise?

    f Why can't Joe Gould watch Max Baer's fight?

22 The writer includes a description of the fight between Max Baer and Primo Carnera. Why? What effect does this scene have? Discuss your opinion with another student.

Chapters 8–9

Before you read

23 Which of these do you think will happen in the next two chapters?

    a Jim leaves his job at the docks.

    b Mae tries to make Jim stop fighting.

    c Jim loses his next fight.

    d Jim becomes the challenger for the heavyweight title of the world.

While you read

24 Match the speakers with the words.

    a "Put it on your eyes."   Jim Braddock

    b "Why didn't you tell me you were going   Joe Gould
        to win again?"   Joe Jeannette

    c "You said it was one fight."   John Henry Lewis

    d "I'll get him a fight if it's the last thing   Mae Braddock
        I do."   Max Baer

    e "You've been training, Jimmy."   Mike Wilson

    f "I can't win if you don't support me."   Rosy Braddock

    g "He isn't the same guy."

    h "The guy's a loser."

After you read

25 Answer these questions.

    a Why are the men at the docks surprised to see Jim?

    b Why is Mae surprised at Joe's apartment?

    c Why is Joe Jeannette surprised when Jim starts training?

    d Why is the radio announcer surprised during the Lasky fight?

26 Imagine Mae's thoughts as she returns home after seeing Joe Gould in New York. Make notes; then have this conversation.

    Student A: You are Mae. Tell Jim about your visit to Joe's apartment.

    Student B: You are Jim. Ask questions. Say what you think about Joe and about Mae's visit.

Chapters 10–11

Before you read

27 In the 1930s, some people with no money lived in New York's Central Park. What do you think life was like for them?

28 In Chapter 11, Jim Braddock meets the champion, Max Baer, outside the ring. What do you think happens?

While you read

29 Circle the correct word.

    a Jim gives money back to *Joe Gould/the Newark relief office*.

    b He buys some *flowers/chocolates* for Mae.

    c Sara tells Mae that *Jim/Mike* is missing.

    d Jim looks for Mike *in Central Park/at the Newark docks*.

    e *A lot of/Few* people go to Mike's funeral.

    f Sporty Lewis asks *Mae/Jim* questions.

    g *Joe Gould/Jim Braddock* asks Jimmy Johnston to stop the film of Baer's fights.

    h *Max Baer/Jim Braddock* tells his opponent, "I don't want to hurt you."

    i Mae throws *a drink/a punch* at Max Baer.

30 Pick one of these people. Imagine what they are thinking at Mike's funeral. Discuss it with a partner.

Jim   Mae   Sara

31 Do you know the complete story of Cinderella? Tell the story. Explain the meaning of the name "Cinderella Man."

32 Work in pairs. Act out the conversation between Jim and Mae after they have met Max Baer at the club.

Student A: You are Mae. You are afraid that Jim will get badly hurt or killed. Ask him not to fight Baer.

Student B: You are Jim. Tell Mae why you have to fight and try to make her feel better.

Chapters 12–13

Before you read

33 It is time for the big fight. How do you think these people feel about it?

Jim   Mae   the Braddock children   Jim's neighbors   Max Baer

While you read

34 Are these sentences true (T) or false (F)?

a Joe Jeannette thinks that the champion's ribs are weak.   . . . . .
b The champion is heavier than the challenger.   . . . . .
c Jim's children are at their aunt's house during the fight.   . . . . .
d Mae stays to watch the whole fight.   . . . . .
e Max Baer is worried in the first round.   . . . . .
f Baer breaks Jim's ribs in the second round.   . . . . .
g The champion stays calm in the fight.   . . . . .

After you read

35 Discuss these questions.

a What helps Mae to change her mind about the fight?
b How is Jim Braddock's attitude to boxing different in 1935 than it was in 1928? Explain your answer.

Chapter 14

Before you read

36 How do you think these people will feel if Braddock wins? How will they feel if he loses?

Mae   Ancil Hoffman   Sporty Lewis

37 Who do you think will win the fight? Why do you think that?

While you read

38 Number these events in the correct order, from 1 to 6.

a	Mae listens to the fight with her children.	.....
b	Joe Gould jumps into the ring.	.....
c	The judges' decision is announced.	.....
d	Mae walks away from the radio.	.....
e	Max Baer comes over to Jim's corner.	.....
f	Jim takes Baer's big punch and smiles at the champion.	.....

After you read

39 What was Max Baer trying to do in the fight? How were Jim's attitude and fighting style different from the champion's?

40 In your opinion, why did poor people across the country support Jim Braddock?

Writing

41 You are Sporty Lewis. Write about the Braddock-Baer fight for your newspaper.

42 You are making the movie of *Cinderella Man*. Write a scene when Jim first sees Mae and the children after winning the title.

43 Imagine that you are Mae many years after the big fight. Tell Jim's story to one of your grandchildren in a letter.

44 You write about books for a magazine. Write about *Cinderella Man*, telling your readers why they should—or shouldn't—read the book.

45 You are a sports reporter for the radio and you are going to interview the heavyweight champion of the world, Jim Braddock, before his fight with Joe Louis. Write a list of the ten questions you would most like to ask.

46 Write a character description of one of these people:

Jim Braddock   Mae Braddock   Joe Gould   Mike Wilson
Max Baer

Support your description with examples of the person's words or actions.

47 All of the people in the book are real except Mike Wilson and his family. You are the writer of the movie. Write an e-mail to the filmmakers explaining why you put this character in the story.

48 Think about a time in your life when you had to fight for your beliefs. Describe it in a diary page.

49 What does this book tell you about life in the United States in the early 1930s? Write a description of what life was like for many poor Americans at that time. Include examples from *Cinderella Man*.

50 Professional boxers have to be very fit. Write a weekly exercise program for a boxer or for yourself.

WORD LIST

amateur (n) someone who does something because they enjoy it, not because it is their job

announce (v) to tell people about something officially

boo (n/v) a shout showing dislike of a person or their performance

butcher (n) someone who owns or works in a shop that sells meat

cast (n) a hard cover used to protect a broken bone

challenge (v) to try to beat the best person in a sports event

champion (n) someone who is the best in a sports event

combination (n) in boxing, two or more punches that are put together

cross (n) in boxing, a punch that goes from right to left or left to right

dock (n) the place in a port where things are taken on and off ships

dodge (v) to move quickly so that something doesn't hit you

fist (n) a closed hand

foreman (n) a worker in charge of other workers

funeral (n) a religious service for someone who has just died

heavyweight (n/adj) a boxer from the heaviest weight group; a **light heavyweight** is a boxer from a lower weight group

hook (n) a curved piece of metal used for picking things up

jab (n/v) a quick punch in which a boxer's hand goes straight forward

knockout (n/adj; **knock out**, v) a hit by a boxer which is so hard that the other boxer falls down and can't get up again

nod (n/v) a movement of your head to say yes or to show agreement

opponent (n) somebody who is against you in a sports event

polish (n) something used to make things shine, for example shoes

priest (n) someone who performs religious services in some religions

punch (n/v) a hit with your closed hand

referee (n) someone who makes sure that rules are followed in sports

relief (n) money, food, or clothes given to those who need them; the feeling that you can stop worrying about something

rib (n) one of the curved bones in your chest

ring (n) a square area, surrounded by seats, where boxers fight

round (n) one stage of a boxing fight, usually lasting three minutes

sweat (n/v) liquid that comes from the skin of a hot or nervous person

wagon (n) a strong vehicle with four wheels, usually pulled by horses